HUSH, CHILD

FINDING MY VOICE AND BREAKING THE SILENCE

DALE LYKINS

CONTENTS

Prologue

Let me assure you, this is not a book about pastoring a church. It isn't even a book about being a Christian, although I do attempt to follow the teachings of Jesus. I would hate for readers to close the book and run away for fear I was going to start getting "preachy." Believe me, I understand why you might want to. I am not a big fan of "Christian" books or any of the trite religious entertainment options, like the Christian movie craze that floods the market from time to time. I don't get it. They are just not very interesting and are way too simplistic.

This is a book about the unexpected and unplanned journey that led to me hearing my voice—really hearing it—for the first time. It started with a powerful experience during voice therapy. Voice therapy revealed my inability to relax the multitude of muscles that are involved in proper voice use. This is a story of what lay behind my silenced voice. It is the exploration of why I had become so accustomed to being silent that I didn't realize I was missing anything or that others were missing my voice as well. A pastor who preaches weekly—in my case multiple times each week—really ought to have heard his or her voice before. This is a story of claiming and using that voice. It is a journey toward authenticity. It is about understanding, for the first time, that I had lived someone else's story, a story that had impacted me since the day I was born. Actually, even before that.

This is about a period of time in my life when demons that had stifled my person, leading to a great silencing of my spirit, were all exposed for what they were. Don't run away. I don't mean Biblical demons. I mean forces that were at work in my life and in people who were part of my life who didn't have my best interests at heart. Sometimes those are church people. I find they can be the worst obstructers. Then again, this isn't a story about church people. It is about people who are found in all of our lives in many different places. They are the people who take from us and only give when it benefits them. In that pattern, they perpetrate the silencing of a voice that otherwise was meant to be heard in this world.

I heard mine. It was powerful, and it was deep. When it broke the silence, my spirit was set free to walk in this world. Untied and let go.

PART ONE

LOST

One

REDUCED TO A WHISPER

I t is no fun for anyone to be struck with any kind of illness near Christmas, but doubly so for a pastor. I mean, there just isn't time. There are sermons to be preached and Christmas Eve services to be led. Besides all that, there are the songs, songs that we only sing that time of year.

Every year on Christmas Eve, I lead a Service of Lessons and Carols. The sanctuary is always dimly lit so the lights from the Christmas trees are more vibrant. The choir, in their robes, walk in singing "O, Come All Ye faithful," and I take up the last position in the parade of joy.

I read through the story of God's saving actions throughout history toward a humanity determined to do all we can to make it hard for God to love us. On Christmas Eve, we are reminded that God, amazingly, loves us anyway. In the Christian story, the God of the universe became vulnerable, born in a stable in Bethlehem in the middle of oppression, violence, and treachery, as the story is told. God loves us so much that God will enter our story as a baby.

At the end of the Christmas Eve Service, all of the lights dim until we are gathered in darkness. The Christmas Trees seem to twinkle as several members of the congregation come forward to light their own candles from the ones on the altar and take that flame down the aisles of the church, offering it to those sitting nearby. One by one, each person in the congregation lights their candle and turns to the person next to them so they can do likewise. When the sanctuary is flooded with candlelight, we sing together. Imagine being present in that moment and not having the voice to sing.

"Silent night. Holy night."

A rabbi told me once while giving a tour of a synagogue, "On Rosh Hashanah these walls all fold back to make one large gathering space. That is the day when Jews come out of the woodwork just in case there really is a God. Much like your Christian Christmas and Easter." He is so right. So, on this night that is silent and holy, there is always a crowd.

Every year, though, I would not join in the singing. Every year, I would be sick, and my voice just wouldn't handle it. I wait all throughout the season of Advent in preparation for that moment of light and exuberant song just to stand and either move my lips or hum in my head. Anticlimactic, to say the least.

One year, the sickness that comes every year came early. I started to feel sick and stuffy nosed on election night 2016. I still blame Donald Trump or maybe I blame Hilary Clinton for losing. Which ever, it really was that night. It showed up then and stayed through the rest of the year and beyond.

I was a pastor in a mostly liturgical church. I call it mostly liturgical, because we had liturgical practices and rituals in a denominational book that was approved for use, but if the pastor didn't want to use them, they really didn't have to. Because every church I have pastored follows the seasons of the Church Year, we observed Advent. Advent is made up of those four weeks prior to Christmas when we light a candle in an Advent wreath each week to remind us that Jesus, the Light of the World, is getting closer and that there is more light this week than there was last week. It marks the time leading up to the celebration of Christmas.

Advent is a season when we Christians remind ourselves of the time in our story when God seemed to be silent. At the end of the Hebrew scriptures there is about four hundred years without prophets speaking—no judges, no commandments, no seas parting. God's people were waiting, and they found themselves in captivity, this time in their own homeland. The Roman Empire had imposed its own will and rule.

One of the first hymns I ever remember singing is "O Come, O Come, Emmanuel," which was written in the fifth century. I most often break the silence to begin Advent with its words, "O Come, O Come, Emmanuel, and ransom captive Israel."

As the pastor, I typically choose the songs sung for worship each week. I try not to choose Christmas carols during Advent. After all, it isn't Christmas yet. Advent is about waiting, and I make people wait. It's not like the angels sing "Hark" every week.

In 2016, Thanksgiving came and went, and I was still sick. Coughing had set in—the kind of coughing that makes me feel like my head and face are turning inside out. I sometimes would think my eyes were going to fall out of their sockets. No cough medicine worked. Cough drops made me feel like I was attempting some sort of remedy instead of passively enduring, but they really didn't help either.

When Advent came around, my other cold symptoms were mostly better, but the cough still lingered. I went to the doctor after I had already coughed, sneezed, and snotted my way through eight Sundays. Sleepless nights of stopped up nostrils and coughing had stolen my rest and energy long enough.

The nurse practitioner determined I had an ear infection. I picked up antibiotics and allergy medication at the pharmacy.

After Christmas Eve passed, without me singing the carols—again—my voice started to give completely out.

Normally, my days are filled with talking. I meet with and talk to people all the time. I noticed that, following conversations and ministry team meetings and staff meetings, my voice was hoarse. That had never happened before.

I was also trying to sing in the church choir. Rehearsals were rough. I sang tenor and found myself dropping out more than I liked. I just couldn't hit the high notes. Toward the end of the hour and a half practice, I couldn't sing at all. I just sat and listened, following along with the music so I could at least absorb what was supposed to be sung, assuming I would be able to when the time came. Singing during Sunday worship was usually fine. I just pushed through it and made it work.

This time, though, something was different. I knew this was not going to be sustainable. I was worried about the hoarseness I was experiencing. That was new, and I wondered if something more serious was going on that I didn't know about.

I made an appointment with an Ear Nose and Throat specialist. He looked around with a mirror, and he didn't notice anything unusual that could be causing the problem. He asked if I wanted him to look deeper with a scope, and I said, "No, that's alright. I will just wait and see." He gave me some tips, and I left. However, there was no relief, and it didn't get better.

One Sunday after that doctor appointment, all the weeks of illness came to a head. I guess you could say literally.

The liturgist was sitting in her assigned seat to the side watching. The Choir was behind me watching. The congregation was in front of me watching. I stepped out center stage and started to talk. I was just beginning to preach, just coaxing the congregation into it with some introductory remarks when, out of the blue, the cough showed up, with a vengeance.

I started to cough-the ugly, strained-eyes-popping-out-of-sockets kind of cough. It wouldn't stop. I took a drink of water. I coughed in mid-swallow. Water spewed out of my mouth. My eyes were wet from the strain. Snot came out of my nose. Everyone, including God, just had to sit and watch. My face was red from the exertion and the embarrassment of having everyone watch my struggle on full display. If I was any kind of good pastor, I wouldn't show my weaknesses, right? I would be in control of everything that happens, right? I was mortified. I couldn't even control my own mucus, much less anything else. The liturgist handed me tissues (always a staple near any choir and church pulpit). I blew my nose, got more water, and finally, the coughing jag came to an end. I did my best to compose myself and preach.

The next day, I made an appointment with my family doctor. He tried some more antibiotics and told me that I was to be on absolute voice rest for the rest of the week. That meant no preaching the coming Sunday.

Thanks to the willingness of a person in the congregation who stepped up and delivered the sermon I had written for the next week with ease and grace and power, I was the liturgist and mostly watched. I was silent during the singing of hymns.

By March, I still wasn't any better.

After yet another trip to my general practitioner, I went to another otolaryngologist, and that time I finally got some answers. Dr. Brorard suggested looking at my throat with a scope, and I agreed. The process can't be done unless the throat is numb. It's done by spraying Lidocaine out of a can and through a flexible tube inserted into the nose. Not fun. However, it gave us the picture that helped turn the corner. Dr. Brorard suggested that I see a specialist in their practice, Dr. Giliberto, who worked with voice issues. I made the appointment before I left.

Two days later, I was sitting in a chair talking with Dr. Giliberto. Another scope, this time with a video camera, was highly suggested. That meant more Lidocaine out of a rubber tube up my nose. I remarked that I had just had that done two days ago, to which Dr. G said, "I agreed to get scoped seventeen times one day to teach students the technique." He was offering no sympathy.

Dr. G had me watch the video screen as the scope intruded into my throat, and I admit, it was pretty cool seeing the inside of my throat and how it all worked. He had me make sounds while we watched the monitor. Different sounds made my vocal cords do different things, showing the range of the issue.

The test revealed the diagnosis: paresis. My two vocal cords, more appropriately called vocal folds, were not meeting in the middle. I had never really thought about what it takes to make the sound that comes out of my mouth. To do that ordinary, common, and often used skill, vocal folds vibrate hundreds of times a second. They kind of beat against each other in the center of the larynx. The vocal folds make that motion up to 1300 times per second for a soprano, for instance. Vocal folds can be hard workers. Mine were meeting to make sound but over to one side rather than in the center. One of the cords was paralyzed, sort of, and the other one was picking up the slack and stretching farther than would be normal to meet the other. After repeated use, that one vocal cord was getting tired. That was the cause of the hoarseness.

It was a relief to have an answer. Apparently, some upper respiratory infections can cause this paralysis. The infection I just had was the Grinch that stole Advent, Christmas, Epiphany, and Lent, and it was reaching out for a rapidly approaching Easter. No "Hark the herald Angels Sing." No "Angels We Have Heard on High." And, it seemed clear that there would be no "Christ the Lord is Risen Today." I would have to find a way to celebrate the central idea of my faith in silence.

I could imagine stepping forward at the beginning of the Easter worship service, raising my arms and proclaiming with a pitiful whisper, "He is risen!"

Two

LOST IN EVERYONE ELSE

Pastoring a church can be an amazing thing. I get a front row seat watching God work in some surprising ways. At other times, pastoring a church is a bitch. It is hard. After all these years, I have come to expect people to do the worst possible thing, make the unhealthy choice, or act in the most destructive way. I am often the recipient of those delightful outcomes because I am the leader and the face of any change.

I've been called all kinds of names. On one occasion, I showed up at the congregation's Lay Leader's (sort of the Chairman of the Board) house to discuss church matters that had presented themselves. His wife, who was clearly one of the issues, was upset that I showed up at their house to talk to her husband. She told her grandfather, who then threatened to get a restraining order if I came to their house again.

A leader in one congregation came to see me about a young couple who had not been seen at church for weeks.

"They are upset with you," he let me know. "They are hurt."

My mind raced back to a moment a few months prior.

Some people will come to talk to me and not take one bit of direction I give. Often, they only want me to help them feel good about themselves and to soothe their dilemma with some prayer, give them that exact word that will change everything back to normal, whatever that is, like a drug. It's never that easy. I can't say a prayer and fix everything. I'm a preacher, not a magician. Maybe if I were a magician, I wouldn't still be dealing with my own emotional baggage after all these years. Poof! It would just go away. I find, even in my own life, that God rarely works that way. Healing and wholeness take a lot of work and effort. It is intentional, and it is difficult. If I want things to get better, I know I'd better be prepared to work for it.

So, I tell people the truth. "I wish I could just make this go away or there was an easy answer, but there isn't," I remind them and myself. "But there is one thing we are promised and one thing that is always true. No matter what we are going through or dealing with, God is with us," I say. And, I believe that more than I believe anything else. It is the core of the Christian story. It is the reason I still hang on and go at it each day, this job of ministering. It may be all I can say, but it is the most powerful thing to be said. That proclamation has repeatedly changed my life, and I have watched it change others. I have come to realize that is my job—to remind the world that God is here. In some way that I don't understand fully, God remains forever God-With-Us. Advent, Christmas, and Epiphany have become my favorite times of the year, because they are the most powerful parts of the story, in my opinion and experience. Advent calls us to wait as we are promised God is coming, and God shows up in mysterious ways. Christmas celebrates that moment of vulnerability when God showed up as a naked baby. Epiphany is that season that tells us the Light of God shines to all the world, even to people we had marked off our list.

But some will say, what about the redemption, and the cross, and the resurrection, and the Holy Spirit, and heaven, and sin? You know, SIN? Without God showing up, none of it matters or would be all that transformative.

By the way, when it comes to that sin thing, we make way too much of it. In my early life, I was taught sin was all about what I did. Dancing was sin. Listening to rock music was sin. Smoking was sin. Drinking alcohol was sin. Having sex was sin. Cussing was sin. Going to the movies was sin. Watching television was even a sin in some of my friend's churches. For some folks, wearing short sleeves was sin. It's depressing and has little to do with anything, except that it is one more way we humans take a message of freedom and life and make it about restriction and death. That we Christian folks have taken good news and made it such bad news is the real sin, if you ask me!

Where in that list is greed? How about how we treat others, like the stranger in our land? Where is that sinful act on the list? How are we at loving our neighbor? I now think sin is anything that blocks me or others from living a full life as a child of God.

Even still, I have seen glimpses of hope. I've seen people surprise me and show kindness. I have seen people make the decision to love. I've seen spouses put their marriage back together after unfaithfulness. I've seen people move on from bad relationships and find a whole new lease on life. I've watched groups of leaders make decisions that promoted healthy ways to be a community of messy humans. I've seen folks return to find open arms had been waiting for them, watching for them.

As a pastor, there are times I get to watch that. Mostly though, I get to agonize over how rarely and to what small extent folks get that. I also have been the recipient of their cruelty when they choose fear and act that out instead of love. Recently, I was called a hypocrite and a liar, and that was by a church staff person. I was asked to share my thoughts, only to have them picked apart and deleted like lines on an edited page. Those days are all too often the case. People, myself included, act out of fear more than anything else. When other's fear and my fear meet, it is hell.

Those are the moments when I think, "I don't want to do this job any longer. I am tired of dealing with this."

One church goer once said to me at the door of the sanctuary following worship, "You are the worst thing that has ever happened to this church." I had just poured my heart and soul and energy out to give voice to the message inside me, and that was the response. Nothing else that day mattered. Those words were all that stuck. "You are the worst thing!"

I was extremely aware when working with that congregation that I was always being evaluated. After those kinds of comments and feeling as if people were always judging me, it was easy to want to keep my head down and stay quiet. The comment that morning reinforced a belief that had lodged deep within me since childhood, that my voice was not welcome or appreciated. I believe a culture of fear can arise within churches. There is a fear that some idea will change the status quo. That is one of the biggest challenges to church folks, the fear that someone else's idea will be used and another will lose out. People want their voice heard above all others. What they don't want is to listen to something that challenges them.

Three

TAKE A BREATH

Dr. G. decided that I should try voice therapy before going the route of surgery. He thought the voice therapist could help me strengthen my paralyzed vocal fold.

In an exam room with the voice therapist, Renee, I heard my voice for the first time. It took me 54 years, but it finally happened. Renee held my waist as I stood with my feet firmly planted on the floor. She was making sure that I followed her direction showing me how deep she wanted me to breathe. She coached me to fill my lungs, breathe through the diaphragm, and fill my back with air. Deep breaths would give the support I needed. Once the air was present, I could just let it happen. The sound would rise up and come out, she assured me.

I couldn't imagine. I have never been relaxed enough to just let anything just happen in my life. I had to work at it. I had to push it out. I had to make it happen, or it wouldn't happen. All that pushing and making and striving caused tension in my body. I carried emotional stress in my muscles. That was something I suspected, but it became clear during this process. Tension and stress had become part of me. When

I used my voice, I did it with constriction and force. I never realized how much that was true until these moments.

I did it though. I trusted my therapist. I breathed in, deeply. She encouraged me, "That's it!" I felt my being fill up, creating a reservoir of air from which to draw. My mouth opened to read the words, "When sunlight strikes raindrops in the air, they act as a prism and form a rainbow ... When a man looks for something beyond his reach, his friends say he is looking for the pot of gold at the end of the rainbow."

It happened. I heard it loud and clear, yet it felt like I had exerted zero effort. I hadn't forced the sound out. I hadn't tried to raise the volume. I had just opened my mouth and let it out. It pierced my soul. That was my natural, unforced voice. It was full and powerful and commanding. I wept. I had never heard such a beautiful, powerful sound. Nor had I understood how far down my own voice, my true voice, had been hidden and suppressed—blocked by years of doubt.

Renee had me sit in a chair in front of a mirror to practice a vocal exercise and see what it looked like. While I was doing that, she left the room to make a copy of an instruction sheet for an exercise she wanted me to work on.

When she came back in the room, she said, "How'd it go?"

"It didn't," I said. "I've been crying this whole time."

It was one of the most powerful moments of my life.

I was not sure exactly when it happened that my voice became restricted. I was not sure of the moments that contributed to the way I moved through the world with my muscles constricted into a tightness that choked the breath right out of me. I was not sure if there was any one moment that hid the power of my own voice from my consciousness. However, I did know that I was ready to claim the pot of gold that had been beyond my reach. I wanted to hear more of this beautiful sound that was me.

At the outset of our sessions, Renee asked me how I used my voice on a daily and weekly basis. It was the first step in a long-term plan to get me through this. She knew I was a preacher, so that was one major use of my voice each week. At the time, I was preaching three worship services that ran from 8:30 in the morning to noon every Sunday. I sang at least three hymns and up to five contemporary songs during those worship services. That is a total of singing eleven songs every Sunday morning. I also sang tenor in the traditional choir. I read scripture. I talked to people between the services. Add to that the scheduled meetings and the impromptu meetings and conversations that occurred on a daily basis in the office, and I was talking a lot.

There was also the singing in the car. I love to sing in the car. I am like Jerry Maguire belting out "I'm free falling…" driving down the road.

"Stop singing in the car," she said with certainty. She told me I could hum. Apparently, humming is always good.

Renee told me right away that I was to go on complete voice rest ten minutes out of each hour every day. People coming into my office during my quiet time were met with a button, meant to pin on my shirt, that I had propped up in my business card holder. The button, from University of Cincinnati Health, announced, "I'm on VOICE REST, so I cannot speak." It was kind of fun, although not easy for a person who talks a lot. I imagined using the button whenever I just didn't want to talk to people!

I told everyone who worked with me what was going on. I made an announcement to the entire congregation about this new reality. They would not see me sing for weeks, and I wanted them to know why. In meetings, whether with large groups or just one person, I was quieter. I didn't talk as much. I bowed out when I felt vocal fatigue. When asked to pray and my voice was tired, I would let it be known, "Can someone else pray? I need to rest my voice." That practice also helped to dispel the myth that only an ordained person can pray when a group of church folks gather.

Handling these situations this way was never a problem. People stepped up and surrounded me with care and understanding. They watched out for me. They took over when I couldn't speak. Some Sundays people would encourage me. "Good voice-use today," a doctor in the congregation said. "You cleared your throat a lot today. You aren't supposed to do that," a caring woman said one week.

Renee said to me at that first appointment, "You don't have to fight to be heard. You, Pastor Dale, have something to say. People want to hear it. You don't have to try so hard to be heard."

As I rested my voice more and started to be quieter in every area of my life, I realized not only how much I hammered away with my voice, but also how intensely I used my words. I was in situations where I talked a lot, as I said, but I also learned that I was hard on my voice. I spoke with hardness and strain. It was as if I was trying to get people to listen with emphasis and volume I put into my words. Not yelling, rather speaking in a way that forced my words out.

Renee also asked me what kind of microphone I used when I was in worship. I told her it was the over the ear version like Britney Spears used, back when people knew who Britney Spears was.

"Since that's the case, think about it like this: you don't have to project your voice to the back of the room when preaching in order to be heard. You only have to get your voice to here," she put her hand to the side of her mouth.

Scales fell from my eyes! What an "aha" moment of clarity. Why had I never thought of that before? That's right! How could I have missed that? All of my preaching life, for nearly 30 years, I have asked my sound crew to turn my mic volume down so that I could "have somewhere to go." I get louder when I preach. Not in the "hellfire and brimstone" kind of angry pulpit pounding. That's never been my style. But to emphasize a point and show I'm excited about what I am saying, I raise my volume. Renee was saying that I needed to rely on the microphone to do the work of projecting volume. I needed to talk. Normally. Like I'm talking to my own cheek next to my mouth. No louder. The amplification system in the room would do the projecting.

That very week, I met with my sound crew and told them about my new revelation, which would require more attention from them. They helped to reset my sound level. I then asked them to pay attention to my sound needs as I went along. I had to trust them if this new method was going to work.

When I needed to make a point in a sermon that was crucial, I could emphasize my words with actions, gestures, a softening of my voice volume even. There were other ways, apparently, than just getting louder. I started to incorporate them into my preaching, and it worked.

During my visits to Renee, we started watching videos of my sermon from the previous Sunday. Renee would point out ways I forced my words, tightened up, and talked with tension in my entire body. I could see it as I watched with her. I could hear it. I never noticed before how much I was trying so hard to make myself be heard. It was as if I had to convince people I had a right to be talking. I had to perform in a way that

Four

USING SOMEONE ELSE'S VOICE

My wife and I moved in June of 2019. Our new home had a deck on the back. The previous renters apparently never cleaned out the area under the deck, and I could see why. That type of chore is never pleasant. Who wants to get under there and crawl around? There are the bugs hiding and waiting to crawl on you or bite. One day, months after moving in, I got up the courage to go under there and get the job done. Someone had suggested that I leave the trash, clutter, firewood, and other abandoned items and put lattice around the bottom of the deck and cover it up. Out of sight, out of mind. That was not acceptable to me. I wanted, I needed, to know it was cleaned out. Even though it was the end of summer, I put on long pants, a long-sleeve shirt, a hat, and work gloves. I knelt down beside the mess and made the final decision to go in. I pulled out things I didn't know I would find. There was an old discarded welcome mat. There were children's toys and dog toys. There was old firewood. Sticks. Boards. Empty candy wrappers and Dorito bags.

I had no idea when I began voice therapy in 2016 that it

would impact my life as deeply as it did. It was a lot like cleaning out that mess under the deck. Once I started, I found so much more than expected. You could say I was a mess. There were layers of discarded memories and experiences that, while surprising at times, had still clearly impacted and influenced me and my decisions.

In the fall of 2017, I began to experience an uneasy feeling. I guess you could call it angst. I'm not sure what it was, but I do know it had me questioning much of my life and my leadership and even my ability to accomplish my vision. I was pastoring a mid-sized church and leading a staff of 16 people. Things were fine on the surface, but I felt like I wasn't getting where I thought the church should go. I had shared a vision and it was resonating but not taking off. There wasn't the systematic change that I had hoped for.

I realized that I was being indecisive. I would talk to a key assistant staff person about where we were going as an organization, and they would come up with ideas that seemed good, even though they didn't quite get where I wanted. "Let's give it a try," I would say and then wonder if that would work in the long term. I thought maybe they were right, maybe I was going too fast, and going slower may be the way to make it all happen in the end … eventually.

The result was less action moving the organization toward our shared vision. It ended up reinforcing business as usual. Good things were done. Many things started. That felt good to some folks, but I was floundering in a desire to see a new kind of expression of church and not seeing it materialize. I wasn't getting where I wanted and where the church leadership board had affirmed, even after years of trying.

I finally discovered that one staff member, in particular, was a pro at keeping me and others and the organization in this state of limbo. I wanted to be bold and go to new places. She wanted to play it safe and keep us all in the familiar spaces we already knew. She valued everything in its place where she could make sense of it and categorize everything. She loved flow charts. For the first six years of working together, I appreciated that kind of flow-chart thinking, because I am not that person. Someone has to be, right? Someone has to keep things moving in an orderly fashion. Someone must close the loops. But, I started thinking that the loops don't always need closed. Everything does not need to be categorized. Flow charts can't capture the dynamic of life and fresh expressions.

However, that way of thinking didn't fit into the expectations of those who were above me in the food chain, the upper management that organizes life in a denominational church. So, I suppressed it. I pushed it under the deck. I let it lay there. I questioned my own thoughts and ideas.

Just like every reality television show that tries to save a failing restaurant or business, I found out it was the management that was the problem. I needed to change. And, just like those shows, the realization of that truth was a surprise. That may not be exactly right. I suspected it was me who needed to change, but I hoped I could make minor adjustments and things would get better. They never do. There is no way around it. Chewed up, abandoned, and dirty dog toys do not get picked up from gross, dark, spidery places unless you put on your long pants and go after it. No one else will do it, and no one else can do it.

I was losing my voice, metaphorically as well as physically, even with my own staff. I was letting other people define the path to my vision, which we had embraced and affirmed. Yet, we weren't there due to my acquiescence to fear and passiveness. I had indeed thrown the Doritos bag under the deck so I would not have to deal with it. It bought me more time. In the meantime, I was losing time and my very soul. It became unmotivating to be shot down at every crucial turn.

Don't misunderstand me, I am not blaming all of these issues on one other person. I take the responsibility head on. I was not speaking with clarity. I was not leading with conviction. I was letting someone else drown out the rest of us, including myself, who were ready to go. To add to the situation, this was a person who was more concerned for people like herself, who were comfortable in the traditional model of congregational life and were fearful that would go away. I, along with others, were pulled into her fear. In my quietness, I allowed someone else to speak for me. I gave in. My voice was silent.

And everyone suffered, whether it was seen that way or not. Instead of doing what we felt called to do, we were stuck in "good-enough" mode. Instead of going forward with an all-in commitment to our vision, we were protecting what was default. I began to realize that I needed to make some changes. I had been in that place for nearly six years and felt it might be the last chance to roll out a strategy to get where we were aiming for. We had tried several times before, but our efforts didn't go far enough, didn't go all the way. You only get so many opportunities. This was my last one, and I felt that in my body.

I knew that I needed to gain insight and direction for my future. What was it that I needed to be doing? What was I going to focus on? In my world I would say, "What was God asking of me?" I needed to listen. I needed to rest. I needed to take specific intentional time to figure out what I was going to do with this angst and restlessness. How could I be a better leader, boss, pastor? Who was I really?

Five

I WAS NOT FREE

"Don't run over your audience. Right now, it seems, you come at them like boom, boom, boom," Renee emphasized by smacking the back of one hand into the palm of the other. "Give them time to digest what you are saying."

There was no way to do any of that without learning to breathe and learning to let my voice come out of my core. That was very different from what I had ever done. We worked more on breathing. We always worked on breathing. It was so foundational and yet gave me so much trouble. It was difficult to relax my muscles in my neck and shoulders to breathe deeply as I was being asked to do.

Through my voice therapy, we worked on projecting my voice in healthy ways with full supported breath, letting it come out naturally with all of its own power. One technique for accomplishing that was to picture speaking to an object outside of myself. Not to get louder but to remind myself that is where my voice needed to go. This helped relax my muscles to allow for the air to carry the sound of my voice into the room. Focusing on an object outside of myself helped me to direct my voice across the room—not louder, but with confidence. When using my voice correctly, without the tightness and restraint that I had been, there was a natural depth and volume. Focusing on an object across the room reminded me to open up and just let it out.

To demonstrate and give me a simple tool to practice with, Renee suggested I hold up a finger and twirl it as I speak.

"Speak to your finger," she would suggest. That was amazing and actually helped. While preaching a sermon, I started to speak to the candles on the communion table or the brass cross sitting on that table. I use my hands when I talk. I even make gestures while talking on the phone. I learned to incorporate this hand twirling into that behavior to remind myself to speak forward with confidence and lots of air. Since I was going to make a hand gesture any way, I might as well just twirl it a bit. No one else knew, but it did help me remember my lesson and new practices.

In subsequent weeks, when we watched the sermons on my phone, I could see marked difference in what was happening. I felt it too in the moment of delivery each Sunday. I carried myself differently. There was more grounding. It is as if I was sure of the words coming out of my mouth. I trusted them. I was allowing them to come out of my core. I slowed down and came across more confidently.

People in the congregation noticed. One man who has trouble understanding every word at times because of a hearing loss said he could understand me much better. It was all because I was being more intentional, less forceful, letting go of making something be heard and trusting that it was worth listening to.

The voice therapy also began my relationship with a kazoo. Apparently, kazoos are multi-use, amazing, magical instruments that can be used to solve all kinds of problems.

A kazoo can't make sound unless you are blowing enough air from your core and through a buzzy vibration feeling in your face. You cannot restrict air in your throat and play a full-sounding kazoo song. Relaxing enough to let that happen required me to let go of years of tightness, stress, and control. How much I was constricted became a revelation throughout this experience.

Renee had given me exercises to do on the kazoo, requiring me to repeat them five times each day. The exercises consisted of a comfortable sustained note just to get warmed up. Next was a high pitch, followed by a low pitch, then a scale from low to high, a scale from high to low. All of that was finished off with a song. The song choices included, "Row, Row, Row, Your Boat," "Happy Birthday," "When the Saints Go Marching In," "Take Me Out to the Ballgame," and "Amazing Grace." I always assumed that was thrown in since I was a pastor.

I experimented with each of the songs but landed on "Row, Row, Row, Your Boat," since it was the shortest one on the list. After all, this was five times each and every day, and I had other things to do. Besides, my dog would go crazy. She would pace around the room trying to get away. Sometimes she would make sound along with me. She sat just inches from my face and stared, looking as if she were willing me to have mercy on her.

I did the exercises religiously. I was determined to get better, and they were the first step. I could tell the difference when I finished from when I started. My voice was a bit lower, more easy, relaxed, and full. I was getting it. The kazoo forced me to use air through my lips in a certain way. It relaxed my vocal cords. It left behind that buzzy feeling that apparently you should be looking for. Air was going to the right places, from the core of my body to my face, specifically the lips.

I was surprised at how much of my time with Renee in voice therapy was spent learning how to blow the kazoo. It was hard for me. Relaxing enough to make the sound consistent was difficult. I held so much tension. Honestly, I knew that, but didn't know how much before I was forced to go through this journey. There was another challenge. Relaxing enough to be a little silly looking was not my normal cup of tea. There we both were, Renee and me, sitting in a room in a medical building, playing kazoos together. Yes, Renee was right in there with me. She did with me whatever she asked me to try. She sat there in her white coat looking all official, blowing a kazoo with me. Other times, we would blow air through straws into a cup of water, both of us making sliding scales or blowing a tune through our straws. Bubbles would splash water out of the cup onto us at times.

It sounds fun. It was at times, and yet, letting go and being free enough to do what I was asked was a hurdle.

During the kazoo-blowing drills in particular, Renee would stop to watch and listen. I would do alright for a time, but there always came that moment when the sound was not right or just not coming out at all. In those moments, Renee would point out that it was all about relaxing. We spent time relaxing my neck and shoulders. She gave me neck and shoulder roll exercises to do to help me relax my upper body, as well as diaphragmatic breathing exercises. I added those to my kazoo work.

Relax the shoulders. Open the throat. Breathe deeply into the diaphragm. Let the air come out unrestricted through the face. Specifically, the lips. All of this preparation to speak. Who knew it was so much work?

It was clear to me that the problem with my voice was

exacerbated by years of holding tension in my neck and shoulders. That was my brick wall. I started noticing how much I tensed up my shoulders and neck and throat, and I made a life-altering discovery. I was in a constant state of tension. Holding my muscles tight, stressed, and inflexible had become normal for me over years. I had not fully realized how much of my body I held in this state. It was as if I were protecting my whole being from a danger to come at any moment. I realized that I wouldn't fully get my voice back until I let go of whatever it was that I was protecting myself from. Maybe it was from a sense of not trusting myself. Being scared to let go. Not wanting to put myself out there. Or, not wanting to do it wrong and disappoint Renee.

During the time all of this was taking place, there were memories I had lived with for as long as I could remember that started poking through. These memories had cropped up from time to time for decades, but at this moment in my life, they seemed different. Now they seemed part of a process of discovery that had opened up for me. I began to question their presence in my catalogue of childhood experiences. They seemed out of place for a boy the age of each memory. They began to make me feel uncomfortable, to say the least. I had a feeling there was more to each one than I had ever admitted or acknowledged. The memories would flash into my consciousness at odd times. In the shower I'd have a flashback to a picture frozen in my brain, a familiar scene, one that now made me wonder what was behind it. I think I knew for years that something was wrong, that there was more behind them. I think I knew now that I needed to explore them further no matter what I'd find once I got into them. Perhaps, there was more than I had even been aware. After all, they were just my memories, and they seemed normal to me. Doesn't every boy have a memory of playing sexual games at five years old?

PART TWO

OUTCAST

Six

REMEMBERING

I walked down the carpeted hallway passing numbered offices on each side. The walk was familiar. I had seen Linda for twelve years off and on, although she had been in a couple of other offices during that time. She joked that she wasn't going to send my file to storage after having to retrieve it too many times. It just never closed. I wonder what the label on it says? "Dale Lykins-Perpetually Open Case"? Maybe. Linda has been a literal God-send to me. She is one of many people who comprise the village that gives me support and keeps me growing. From August 2017 through January of 2018, I walked this hallway weekly.

Fifteen years previously, I had been referred to therapist Linda Six because she took a holistic approach to counseling. Over those years, I worked with her on several occasions. The longest period of time was one year. That entire year, using Eye Movement Desensitization and Reprocessing (EMDR), we worked through many memories that were disturbing or traumatic. Linda and EMDR have been life savers. Through this approach, I have been able to bring closure to many dysfunctional moments, associate more positive emotions with those memories, and release their effects of stress and tension on my body.

***

EMDR was discovered by Francis Shapiro in 1987. While walking in the park, she discovered that eye movements seemed to help decrease negative emotions from her own distressing memories. She wondered why this seemed to be the case and found that the rapid movement of her eyes while thinking of a disturbance helped the disturbance go away. The theory behind EMDR (as explained on the website emdr.com) is that when a traumatic or very negative event occurs, information processing may be incomplete, perhaps because strong negative feelings or dissociation interfere. When the individual thinks about the trauma, or when the memory is triggered by similar situations, the person may feel like she is reliving it, or may experience strong emotions and physical sensations.

The first thing that Linda does to prepare for EMDR therapy is to make a list (set up protocols) of the memories associated with the trauma. During this phase, each memory is evaluated ahead of time for what emotion is associated with the memory and where in the body the patient feels the memory. For me, the abdomen, legs, and neck are typical places I hold my feelings about traumatic moments from my past. After all memories on the list have been reviewed for these details, Linda then will choose one to start with. When we begin, I am seated in a chair across from her. She hands me a headset to place on my ears from which come ocean sounds or soft instrumental music, washing back and forth from one ear to the next. At this point Linda has me start to relive the memory. It is surprising how emotional this can become. It is as if I am right back in the moment, even though

I am always aware of what is happening around me, being in her office, feeling her presence, and hearing her words.

As we work through the feelings associated with the chosen memory, my younger self (usually the case) is encouraged to express whatever needs to come out. I am often amazed at how much anger is held inside over, in many cases, decades. Once the feelings are expressed completely, Linda will ask again where in my body I feel this memory. Then she will ask me what positive emotion I now associate with it.

We started building the protocol list with the vagina memory and then moved on from there to Papaw running his finger across my butt. Those seemingly small, insignificant pictures from my past that flash through time were anything but small in significance once their power was unleashed. I broke down in tears mentioning each one. I told Linda about playing a record player at night, and my body reacted. I became tense. I cried. It was clear there was so much more to it than that. Just mentioning it elicited an emotional response from me. That happened time after time. I'd say, "I don't know what this means and why I am putting it on the list or bringing it up, but I remember…"

Seven

WHO KNEW?

Why would a little boy have these memories? How does a little boy know things to say to a five-year-old friend that would make him run away in disgust? Why does thinking of peeing outside make me tense my shoulders and upper body like I'm preparing to protect my body from danger or to endure something both familiar and epic?

All of the memories on my list were ones that just hung around seeming to be normal. However, looking at them and listing them all together in one place at one time, they seemed to reveal a darkness that was straining against the light of my consciousness. As I walked down the hall to Linda's office, the wall was ready to break open. I was actually anticipating the journey because, like in times past, I knew there was a healthier existence on the other side. Still, I did not know how difficult the journey would be.

On the list of memories we were developing protocols for was my friend from kindergarten. His name was Willie. I remember very little about Willie. He is present in a few birthday party pictures from childhood.

In the memory, I was standing at the fence that separated our backyard from Willie's backyard. Willie was on the other side. I asked him something. I don't remember what I asked him. I do remember his response. With all the shock a kindergartener can muster, Willie replied, "No! That's nasty."

Then, he walked away.

Linda and I spent time on the memory of a metal shed that sat in the far corner of my parents' backyard. I have clear memories of being in the shed, door shut with my pants down. Was I alone? The memory I have always seen in my mind doesn't include another person.

I remembered Papaw peeing in the backyard. My grandparents on my mother's side, Mamaw and Papaw, lived out in the country in the small town of Beaver, Ohio, so it's not really all that unusual a concept that he would pee outside. Was that all there was to it? Given all the other memories, I decided to add it to the list.

In one memory from the third grade, I was sitting with everyone else in the school gym for an assembly. The boys around me were talking about their latest game and fun moments. I have no idea what conversation led me to say this, but I do remember saying it.

"I was playing in the bathtub after my grandma washed me."

That went on the list.

Those boys were relentless, like most of the kids I went to school with from that moment on. Laughter broke out, and they couldn't wait to tell everyone else.

"Hey! Lykins' grandma still gives him a bath."

You mean that wasn't the case for everyone? I didn't understand at the time.

During EMDR therapy, the counselor frequently asks the

patient to imagine the subject of the situation (for me, it was the little boy at the age of the memory) in a safe room. The adult me would ask the little boy, "What do you have to say to me?"

"She is not your friend!" came the reply as quickly as I finished the question.

I knew it down deep. Mamaw was not a friend to me. She used me. She touched me when that was not okay. There were other memories. Papaw in bed with me. A flash of one memory of penetration. This was what I had suspected for years and never wanted to know more about, until now.

Even as a kid, sex was part of my life, its presence lurking in the background as far back as my memory takes me. My normal everyday life involved sexual feelings, knowledge, and desires, even before I really understood anything about what all of that meant. I thought that all kids played like I did or had thoughts like I did. But there were moments when it was clear that what slipped out of me on occasions was not something a five or six year old would just know about on their own.

At my grandparent's house, there were several stuffed animals I played with for many years. They had been in the family for a long time, likely my mom's before me, easily discovered and reinvented for my own fantasy world. One was named Whitey. Whitey was a white bear about 18 inches tall who had a maroon tail and paws. I would take Whitey's maroon tail and pull it through to the front so that it stuck out between his legs. I was fascinated by Whitey's maroon dick. Seems innocent, and yet it was such a major part of my play that it also seems out of place.

At one point when I was in fourth grade or so, I went through a sex talk and play period that got to be too much for my cousin, Sandy. She lived just down the country road from

Mamaw and Papaw's house, and we would spend summers together. Even though never physically played out, during this period way too much of my talk was focused on my penis or penises in general. I took any scenario we were playing, like acting out our own episode of "Star Trek," and turned it into dialogue that would include a reference to a penis. Our phone conversations included my sexual references too. One day, she called me on it, and even I realized at my young age that I had taken it too far. I remember making a concerted effort to dial it back.

Later on, my sister, Ruth, and I lived in a fantasy world populated by doll characters, each with their unique personalities and voices and relationships. Her Barbie dolls, Skipper, and an assortment of knockoffs, and my GI Joes, Big Josh, Big Jim, and Johnny Quest made up this eclectic community. We each had our character dolls we "worked" as we called it-meaning providing the voice and actions and expected personality. Each of us had male and female dolls in our allotment. Skipper was mine to work. Skipper was pretty wild. She was sexy. She dressed to draw attention to herself. She had sex. Once Skipper's boyfriend, Josh (who I also worked), was preparing for a night of romance. I fashioned a paper penis for Josh, complete with color from a crayon and brown pubic hair. Skipper was delighted.

Those are examples of moments in my life that stand out as windows into an adult world that most children are not a part of—moments that pull back a curtain to reveal exposure to sex at an early age. I never thought a lot about them. They were my life. Then they started to connect and create a picture of a boy and eventually a man in distress.

It took my voice being silenced from a viral paralysis and the journey toward healing that physical condition to realize the depth of stress on my body and spirit. My voice had been so completely silenced over the years, through abuse, fear, control, manipulation, and denial, that I wasn't sure who I was. Who was I without all of the other shit that had infected me from the very beginning of my life?

My papaw used me in ways that broke my spirit. My mamaw took advantage of a child's vulnerability for her own needs to be met. My mom, knowing nothing more or different herself, became caught in the scheme. My dad, through his silence, wasn't there to protect me. My response was to tense up my body. Hold things close to me. Cut myself off from others and the world. Try to control outside forces that threatened me. Deny myself. My voice was disregarded—lost-even to me.

As I learned about my memories and put the pieces together, I became determined that I would not let anyone or anything else take my voice from me again. The connection between that part of my life and what it would take to relax the tension stored up in my body, to heal and use my vocal folds, was coming together.

Eight

SEPARATED

My sister, Ruth, was born in 1966. I was three years old. I don't remember much at all about that time. That may seem typical except that I remember tiny details of clothing, smells, and surroundings, throughout much of my life. But not this time period. I am pretty certain it's because I wasn't around when Mom was pregnant. During that time, I lived with Mamaw and Papaw more than I lived at home with my parents. Giving your kids to someone else to deal with was a pattern for my parents. I was given to Mamaw and Papaw. Ruth was left with the Stephens—Imogene and Harold Stephen were distant relatives on our mom's side of the family. Mom told me years later that she was broken about it inside. She didn't know what to do with me when I was born. She was just eighteen. She had never been around kids, let alone taken care of one. Even at the age of three, I did not fit into my parents' world.

Once Ruth was born, we were together as a whole family for a few years. I recall a house we all lived in on the south side of Columbus when I was in kindergarten and first grade. Ruth's room was just next door to mine. She was old enough at that point that we played together, as became typical for us when we had the chance. In that particular place in Columbus, we played in the unfinished basement. It had concrete floors and cinderblock walls, but we kept several toys down there. We would also ride our big wheels around and around the central staircase that led upstairs, laughing and screaming with delight.

One favorite toy was a robot that, when turned on, would walk slowly stopping every few mechanical steps to open his chest and shoot 2 guns hidden there. They would light up in red, and a sound would play, adding to the excitement. We would place the robot in the corner and let him walk toward us while we rode our big wheels around and around, the robot getting closer and closer. He would shoot. We would scream. Those were fun times. Mom would yell down and tell us to stop screaming. We would get quiet for a moment. Only a moment.

I remember less about the period between first and fourth grades when it comes to my relationship with Ruth. It was a period of time I was once again living with Mamaw and Papaw, and Ruth was most often with Imogene Stephen, who watched Ruth (and me some too before I went away) while Mom and Dad worked each day.

Over the years, the Stephens had become quite important to my sister's life, and mine as well, even though they understandably were more connected to Ruth. I never stayed with them as much as Ruth had, having lived with Mamaw and Papaw so often. When I was an adult and talking with Imogene about the past, she enlightened me that on some evenings, no one came to pick Ruth back up, so she would stay overnight. Some weekends, she stayed as well. Sometimes, it would be two weeks at a time. The Stephens ended up being like a second family (or maybe even first) to Ruth throughout her life. I know better why that was now.

I don't recall Ruth and I being together at home, where Mom and Dad lived, at all during that time. I remember how we would play together at Mamaw and Papaw's. I remember being with her at Imogene's. I remember being together at Lykins family gatherings. I remember moments, but not in our parents' house. While I lived with Mamaw and Papaw those couple of school years, I would go home to Mom and Dad's (I still called it home) anticipating seeing Ruth. At that time Mom and Dad lived in a townhouse that had one large bedroom Ruth and I shared when we were there. I'd get upstairs to the bedroom and Ruth (more often than not) wasn't there, her bed perfectly made and empty. No toys out. No sign of her, just a girl's bed with a frilly canopy as evidence a daughter belonged there somehow. It was always disappointing.

When I was in the fourth grade, I returned home for good. I had been living with Mamaw and Papaw solidly for over a year. My mom and dad were visiting Mamaw and Papaw for the weekend. It was Sunday, and they were engaged in their ritual of packing and preparing to go home. I was acting out. I ran from room to room in Mamaw's house. My mom wanted to talk for some reason, and I would run to the next room and slam the door just as she was getting close. Finally, my dad, at the urging of my mom, got me to stop. I screamed and cried, and he slapped my face. It worked. I stopped, and we sat down on the edge of the bed I shared with Papaw. I don't remember anything we said, except I do remember asking if I could go home with them. My mom answered that I could once school was out.

After they left, Mamaw was furious with my dad for

hitting me. She usually took my dad's side in everything over my mom. She told me, "When you go to school tomorrow, and the teacher asks about that mark on your face (yes there was one, and yes it was there the next day, and yes Mrs. Schroeder asked), you tell her your dad hit you." I did. I don't think anything else happened.

I returned home at the end of that summer. Ruth and I grew closer once we were living in the same house, to the point that we were almost inseparable. Today we are still close. We know what it is like to be separated and lost to each other.

Nine

DIFFERENT

As a kid, I wasn't part of the in-crowd. I was never part of that coveted group in any school I had ever attended. However, in seventh and eighth grades, years that are full of anxiety and stress for most kids, I excelled at being different. In seventh grade, I wore my mom's pants to school. They were cool bell bottoms that hit me just right showing my platform shoes only slightly at the bottom. I wore chains around my neck, some with medallions. Lots of chains, necklaces, some my mom's. I wore rings on most every finger, yes, a mixture of mine and my mom's. Dressing so flamboyantly—showing off in some way—was an attempt to say something that would get noticed. It was a way to express who I was that even I didn't completely understand.

I was not like the jocks and pretty boys who had the girls fawning all over them. The boys, even I noticed, though silently. I didn't like sports. I didn't like gym class. It showed. I tried, but those hours were dread-filled as I would try to act like the other boys and fail miserably. I never understood it. Nothing I tried was good enough to break the testosterone ceiling. My wardrobe didn't help in this junior high culture that rewarded conformity. At least that is what I assumed. Even when I thought I was acting like them, it would turn into an occasion to tease me about that. I never could break out of the trap. I read and did word search puzzles during study hall. I was quiet, expressing myself through my outer appearance. I still like shirts that invite notice. I'm a pattern and bright colors guy. The older I get, the brightness is being replaced with more subdued colors, but trust me, my personality makes up for it!

Each day after school, I walked to Imogene and Harold's house, the same Imogene who had been watching my sister, in babysitter fashion, since she was a toddler. I would walk out of the school and just across a field to the after school retreat. It was a short walk and it gave me freedom from the teasing. I could go to Imogene's house and feel release and respite from the stress of keeping up the appearance of a got-it-all-together cool kid (I don't think I was fooling anyone, but it was important for me to keep up the act). During the two hours until one of our parents picked us up, we played games and watched television. There was food to eat, even dinner if our parents hadn't picked us up by the time the Stephens were ready to sit down at the table. Imogene and Harold's families were from the same Appalachian region of the state as mine. One indicator was Imogene could cook the food my mamaw prepared really well. I can still taste her awesome fried pork chops and mashed potatoes—the creamiest potatoes ever, never any lumps, paired with a side of applesauce. Even as a young teen, I realized I couldn't keep eating Imogene's food for dinner and then eat again when I got home and mom placed our dinner on the table. I was putting on inches and those pants of my mother's wouldn't fit for long.

One day, the bell rang at the end of the last period. With everyone else, I headed to my locker where I left behind my books and spiral notebooks. I grabbed my jacket and started toward the exit. I was happy to leave. Reaching Imogene and Harold's house, I went straight to the basement, which was finished to provide a family room with a television, a kitchen, laundry, another bedroom, and a bathroom. On a previous visit, I had discovered a chest in a bedroom occupied by Harold's single brother that held a hidden supply of Playboy magazines. The secretive stash interested me so far as it seemed risqué and off-limits more than it provided any sexual provocation. I saw things I had glimpsed or imagined before but never observed in such close proximity or with such boldness.

This time, however, among the Playboy magazines were a couple of Playgirls as well. I took one and went to the bathroom. I didn't really need to do anything in there except close the door for privacy. I eagerly opened the pages and eyed the pictures that immediately captured my attention. There were pictures of naked men with hairy legs and chiseled shaped features that kept me turning to the next page. There was a man lathering up in the shower. The centerfold was a reclined man with not one bit of clothing on his body. I studied that image over and over, fixated on this man that stirred me to attention.

I left the bathroom and went back to the bedroom and tossed the magazine behind the laundry hamper until I could safely come back later to put it away. Then, I went upstairs to get ready for the pork chops.

"Who was looking at this?" Imogene said as she came up the stairs magazine in hand. She was visibly upset. She knocked on each of her adult daughters' bedroom doors and asked if it was them. She asked Ruth. She asked me.

I said, heart beating out of my chest, "No." I just knew, even though it had never been said outright, that I could not admit to the truth.

I had lied about more than the magazine. It certainly wasn't the first time I had lied to deny what was a fact of my life. I could not remember a time when I was not curious, drawn to, or inclined to stare at male bodies. As a young boy, I was fixated on boys' hair, jawlines, or what they looked like behind the bulging pants. I didn't have words to express it, and it was not encouraged to talk about it. It was my secret. They fascinated me. When I saw guys, especially in a group, I felt attracted like someone on the outside of a window peering in so desperately desiring to be included. I was convinced that I didn't belong in the same category. No one else felt like me. Guys liked girls, right? I had convinced myself that's the reason for the teasing and the ridicule at school. I was not like everyone else. Even though not really sure how or why, I was an anomaly needing to push down what I felt in order to survive those awful junior high years.

At this age and stage in my life, though, I really didn't know what I felt. I didn't have a name for it. All I knew was that my eyes found their way to male bodies and features. They always had, for as long as I could remember. I recall words like fag, queer, and gay being thrown at me, labeling me as an outcast, and not really understanding all that they meant other than that I was different, not like the other guys.

That moment of being confronted by Imogene with the magazine was one of many that reinforced the lies that became my strategy for survival, hiding myself like the magazine of nude men thrown haphazardly in a corner. I wonder if it would have been harder for anyone to believe my "No" if it had been a Playboy magazine that Imogene found. I mean, why would it not be me who took a look, right? I dodged suspicion with my answer and the fact that no one suspected a boy would be looking at boys.

It would take me 40 years to have the courage to admit to myself that the day in the basement wasn't only adolescent curiosity, but a glimpse into a reality that has always been true. A reality that had been neither acknowledged nor embraced, a reality that had been pushed down so no one would notice this awful truth. Not my family, friends, or God.

I felt so alone in those years living on the outside, feeling so different that I had no way to process or talk about it. I could never admit the truth. I didn't even know the whole truth, but even so, it would have been unthinkable.

By eighth grade, I was not wearing the jewelry anymore. I was wearing stylish clothes from the boy's department. I had these cool wedge shoes for guys that I just loved. I was trying to fit in, mixed with a bit more maturity and growth. It didn't matter. I still got teased. I was branded forever, at least that's the way it felt at the time. In junior high, my almost-teen body and mind assumed that those people would always be important in my life.

Most days, I left my house out the front door to make the journey to school, which was just down and across one busy street. I walked with my head down only seeing my feet. My shoes were the focus of my attention. This was my default walking posture. Head down, don't look up, and certainly not around at anything. More importantly, not at anyone else. I was convinced that, whenever I heard a group of other students laughing, they were laughing at me. There was no other explanation that ever entered my mind. This head-down life was safer than risking looking at the faces of those doing the laughing.

In some sense, I had good reason to think that was the case. I was a kid who got teased. There were school assemblies where people flicked little rolled up straw papers toward me from behind, accompanied by laughter. There were moments when a finger reached around the side of my head and flicked my ear, and laughter followed. I didn't want to know who it was, though I had a good idea. It was those popular kids who felt entitled to their status. They would keep their grip on the status quo, which put them at the top of the teenage pecking order, anyway they could. Picking on someone who just took it because it seemed natural and right was their way to bully. I was their person. Silent on most occasions, taking the abuse, I walked head down through the school day in a world only as wide as my size nine shoes.

When I did get angry enough to let it out and yell back, even using curse words like I heard them do, it never worked out like I expected. Then they would say the word back in a mocking jeering tone. What kind of world is this when you lose no matter how you react? Silence or cursing, you are still not cool.

There was one teacher in my school experience during this period of life who was a bully right along with the students. Mr. Dotson taught social studies. One period of my day was study hall in Mr. Dotson's room. He would stand in front of the class and watch us read, do homework, occupy ourselves if we were lucky enough not to have anything that had to be completed for another class. I sat in the back row with two other guys who actually were nominally nice to me. At least, we tolerated each other.

The bell rang one day for the period to be over. Mr. Dotson was out of the room talking to another teacher in the hallway. Every row of students, including the two boys next to me, got up and started gathering their books, bags, and items to leave. The three of us in the back row got our things and walked out of the room heading to the next class.

Word came from the other students, "Mr. Dotson is looking for you three."

We made our way back to his room. I was nervous. Even though I had no idea why he wanted to see us, it usually wasn't a good thing. Mr. Dotson was the one teacher who meted out corporal punishment for the entire hallway of seventh grade teachers. What would he say? What was he upset about? I had never been in this kind of a situation. I was usually the darling of my teachers.

"Why did you leave my class before I said you could be dismissed?" Mr. Dotson asked with his looming power.

To be honest, I never remember waiting for him to dismiss us ever before, but I knew I'd better think of something and quick.

"I didn't really think about it. I'm sorry. I had been reading when others started moving and gathering their stuff, and I just absentmindedly left with these guys assuming everyone else was also leaving," I said, which was indeed the truth.

Earlier in the year, one of these same guys had forgotten a handout they needed and asked me if I would go ask Mr. Dotson for another copy as if I had forgotten mine. I was uncomfortable about the request but was thrilled to be included in any scheme, even one so obviously aimed at setting me up and not the real person with a forgetful habit. I did it.

Walking to the front of the class to his desk I said very quietly, "Can I have a copy of the handout? I forgot mine at home," I lied thinking about how this might be an initiation into the club of coolness.

49

Glaring at me, Mr. Dotson said, not quietly, "Well you forgot it huh? It's a good thing the whale remembered to spit Jonah out isn't it?"

I still don't know what the hell he meant by that.

He told us we were to write a one-page essay on why it's important to wait for Mr. Dotson to release us from his classroom before leaving. I went to the library to work on my essay later that day. I wanted to get it over with and out of my mind. I sat at one of the many round tables with molded plastic chairs surrounding it. The setting was as sterile feeling as my existence felt at the time. What was I going to write about that would fill an entire page? Even knowing that I could write with big strokes of my pen and stretch the words out longer to fill the page only helped so much. I still had to turn in an essay or face Dotson's wrath.

Just across the room, not far from where I sat in my isolation, a group of students gathered around a table and sitting in the same plastic chairs. I have no idea what they were working on or what their time in the library entailed. I doubted they were there to write an essay about why it was a good idea to wait in a classroom until the teacher dismissed you. They had each other to share the moment while I sat alone. I finished my paper, putting down some thoughts about safety in waiting for the adult to tell you what was next and when to go where, not really believing it myself, but it would get me out of Dotson's crosshairs. This wasn't really anything new. I had already learned that adults were not always trustworthy. Adults might make you feel trapped. Adults might harm you. Adults could be the ones who scared you into submission. Adults could be the bullies.

The other table of students broke out in laughter befitting a library, neither loud or soft, just that balance of muffled snicker. My face got hot with embarrassment. I wanted to be invisible. Paper complete, I stood up. I looked at my shoes, head down as I walked to the next class period.

English class was chaotic as usual. Mrs. Greene was a first-year teacher, and it showed. She rarely had control of the class. Students talked over her. Paper wads went flying through the air. The popular boys were the worst. They would tease her mercilessly until she was in tears. It was an everyday occurrence only interrupted by the presence of a substitute teacher on those rare days when Mrs. Greene was absent. Maybe she was recuperating. Maybe she was ill from the stress. Maybe she was contemplating a career change.

I hated the class. It wasn't the content. It was a literature class, and I loved reading and listening to discussion about the books we read. Many times, we could choose our own book to do a report on. I typically chose gothic novels. I was into the stories that captured my imagination and took me away from the mess. I even liked Mrs. Greene. She was soft-spoken and gentle—her bad fortune. She would have been served better by a voice more like Darth Vader, a disposition like a drill sergeant, a personality more in line with Margaret Thatcher. She had none of that. Her face even flushed red when she got upset or when the boys made fun of her or played jokes. It was a class straight out of a Dickens image of a school. Although, I would assume the students would have been throttled quickly and thoroughly in Dickens's day. Oh, my mind imagines it now. Gary Buchannan, the one deemed so cute by the girls and so cool by the boys who wanted to be him, with his straight hair that hung in his eyes and a choker that just reached around his neck, bent over the desk, pants down, and swats from a paddle smacking his red ass. That would have served him right.

Gary and all of his circle of friends had very little to do with me. I was one of those kids in junior high who was just around, in the background, minding their business. However, it seemed that the Garys of the early teen world would not let the Dales of that world just be. Fading in the background was just as likely to get you teased. If you weren't part of the in-group, you were fodder for picking on. I longed for friends.

So, there I was in Mrs. Greene's English lit class, fading into the background, terribly uncomfortable with all the noise and chaos, wishing for the bell to ring so I could move on to Mr. Roberts' science class. At least there it was not chaos and people listened to him. Mr. Roberts commanded control of Gary's disruptive presence and others who felt entitled to steal the souls away from the lower life forms in their orbit.

On that particular day, when the bell rang announcing Mrs. Greene's release from her captors, it announced a new lease on life for me too. Gary walked out slightly behind me. I was suspicious. What did this kid want with me? Gary Buchannan never walked with me.

Gary said, "Lykins, you're okay." And with that, he patted my back.

Wow! This was a groovy day (it was 1976, after all).

I stood much taller in the hallway. I'm okay. Did you hear that? Gary Buchannan said I was okay. And, he used my last name to refer to me. That is what the cool kids do, you know?!

He touched me. I am so not in his caste, and yet he touched me and talked to me.

Brenda, a girl I knew from other classes but not well, was on her way across the hall to Mr. Roberts' science class too. "Hey," she said reaching around my back, "This was stuck on you," and she handed me a piece of paper with a loop of scotch tape stuck to the back.

"I'm a FAG," it read.

My spirits crashed. I retreated to the safe place inside my own self where I realized I should always stay.

"Just keep your head down and don't look up," I would not so much say but embody.

That was a posture I kept for many years. I carried the weight of that note stuck on my back through the rest of school and into adulthood. That note was meant to mark me as different. Like a scarlet letter meant to tell the world that I had transgressed, that note said loud and clear, "This one is different."

I walked with my head down much of the time. As a college student, I may not have literally held my head down when I walked, but I walked with little confidence, always assuming people were critiquing me, ready to pull out the scotch tape rolled in a little loop. "Different," they might stick on my back with a pat, feigning friendship and acceptance. I was always waiting for it or, at least, knew that everyone around me thought it. As an adult, I still battle the feeling that everyone is judging me or has figured out that I am not one of them.

I don't think I was all that different from those other junior high students back in 1976. I was insecure. I was stressed over trying to fit in. I liked the same music they probably did. Kiss, Elton John, and Fleetwood Mac. I enjoyed watching movies. George Carlin and Dallas. If they would have taken the risk to talk with me, we would have been friends.

There is no doubt that I had my own struggles too. My parents had split up, and just before starting that school, they had gotten back together. We moved an hour and a half to this new city and new neighborhood with new people. That was extremely hard for this introverted kid. If they had talked with me, we would have shared the common struggle of our human condition. We were all trying to fit in. It's just that some people got to make the rules, and the rest of us were used to enforce the lines drawn to protect the powerful.

PART THREE

CHAINED

Ten

OUT OF SIGHT

I realized that, in the story I had concocted, the woman whose naked body I was seeing was never wet when I pulled back the shower curtain. She also never had a face. Never ever was my memory of more than her pubic region. During the EMDR session, the snapshot came into better focus, and I realized that she wasn't in the shower, and it wasn't my mother. That was the first time I noticed the graying pubic hair. It couldn't be my mother. My mother had been about twenty years old at the time.

Who was this phantom woman who had haunted me for fifty years? Could it be the older woman who was the babysitter?

And then, it happened.

After several sessions, the counselor said to me, "Does the woman have a face?" Seems like a simple question, but it packed a huge powerful punch. Yes, she did. Once I let myself look closer. It's hard to explain, but it is as if I knew all along but was blocking the whole picture. The pain of it was too much, and I wanted to avoid the truth to protect myself.

I knew it immediately. I didn't want to admit it, but there

was no denying what my mind showed me. It was Mamaw. I had to face the reality that the woman who was most prominent in my life had used me for her pleasure at three years old, or possibly younger. It was a rough journey. So deeply hidden, pushed down out of sight, and yet always known in my own unease.

I wept uncontrollably. The counselor asked me, "Are you okay? Do you need to stop?"

I didn't want to stop, and yes, I was okay. Well, as okay as I could be, and yet I knew what she meant.

Still, nothing fit with my assumptions.

So, what does a woman's graying vagina and a split-level house on a run-down street have to do with a story about voice and the journey to find mine? Everything.

Eleven

A BOY WHO IS NOT SAFE

I spent clumps of time at Mamaw and Papaw's, although we just usually called it Mamaw's. After all, it was really her that we went to see. Papaw was there, and that was alright, but Mamaw held the family together with her gravitational force. She, the matriarch, made sure we visited, were fed, and were sent home with loot in the form of food, clothing, and sometimes cash.

Papaw slept in the chair while the television played "Hee Haw." Or, he sat outside in a lawn chair. We had to want to see Papaw most of the time. He did watch television with us in the evenings, but most often we had to go find him. We had to make the choice to sit with him outside in the best weather, as he watched the cars on the road, many times blowing their horns as the driver or passengers waved a knowing "hello." Mamaw and Papaw had lived there for at least 30 years. Chances were good he knew most of the people zipping by.

On one ordinary afternoon spent at Mamaw's house during my childhood, the sun was shining, and the world was warming after the cold drabness of winter. Dark was giving way to light. Birds were bolder with their songs and could be seen searching for extra food to feed newborn appetites. It was that time of year when bees were busy exploring the new flowers, dandelions mostly. Weeds to us are life sustaining nourishment to the small buzzing life of a bee.

Mamaw kept the front door to the house open on days like that. It let in light from outside, after all, and she would never turn on a lamp or overhead light in the daytime if it weren't absolutely necessary. That would be wasteful. So, while the glass storm door kept the birds and bees outside, the wooden inside door was open, allowing the warm light to flood the living room of the small but comfortable house. Spending time with Mamaw was like spending time with myself. It was natural. It always had been. Never questioned. It simply was.

Though the farmland stretched out in every direction beckoning to be explored by my seven year old self, I was not much of an explorer. I preferred the house. It was cozy. It was home, really. It was safe.

My sister Ruth and I did play outside, but not in an adventuring way. I doubt Mamaw would have allowed it. She was one to keep me close. She would have told me some tale of danger to keep me from even wanting to wander into the world beyond the yard where her gaze could watch everything. Although I can't recall those specific tales now, they would go something like this...

"There was a boy once who wandered out of his yard over on Paint Creek, and he was never found. Just disappeared. Don't know what happened to him to this day," she would have explained. And then, every time we passed the alleged yard while driving by the house on Paint Creek, she would point it out. Every time.

"There's where that boy wandered away and never was

found," lest I forget the dangers of leaving Mamaw's side and her gaze.

But this day found Ruth and I inside the house enjoying the outside through the sunny windows and the open door. Although not always the case, our parents were there this day. Mamaw was in the kitchen preparing food as she always did. She could concoct a meal with seemingly little effort. Mom and Dad were sitting at the table while Mamaw worked. I know they weren't helping. No one helped Mamaw in the kitchen.

Ruth and I colored in coloring books, the big 96 crayon box with all the great colors available to us. We often sat on our knees on the floor to color with our butts stuck in the air resting bent forward on our elbows to steady our hands so we could stay in the lines. Childhood innocence warmed the moment like the sun's touch warmed the earth outside.

Papaw was there too, sitting in his rocking chair. It was one of two, hard, scratchy upholstered chairs that were placed in the living room. The one near the front door and television was Papaw's. The other sat alongside the first but in a corner with a bedroom door between them. The orange and brown and gold flowered patterned couch and a matching chair faced Papaw's brown chair. A big picture window took up the majority of one wall.

Papaw sat where he had sat many times before as we colored as we had many times before. Then without warning, Papaw snuck quietly behind us, which wasn't difficult since we were nearly at his feet and deep in concentration on our coloring task. He snuck up from behind and ripped the innocence from the scene.

"Zip," he said, and zip went his index finger through the crack between my butt cheeks, across my anus, to end at the small of my back. He laughed and laughed, proud to pull off his sneak attack, while I was astonished with surprise and unease.

I felt something very uncomfortable had just taken place. I jumped, having been startled, realizing I had been duped. He got me, for sure. I did not like this feeling. It was a mixture of the fright of seeing a ghost and the humiliation of being disciplined at school.

This was the moment I learned I could not trust adults. Perhaps not anyone. No other adult in the house came to my rescue, or even my defense. It was all a matter of a joke played out on an innocent boy, and what harm could there be in that? People mostly tolerated Papaw, and I learned that this is what adults do. They tolerate evil, even when it hides in plain sight on an early summer day and in bright sunlight. There was no hiding. This was bold.

This is one memory that has never left me. Without warning it will abruptly flash across my mind. Like the other adults on that day, for the longest time, I ignored it, brushed it off as a joke. But, 50 years later, it would send me to the counselor one more time. It was no joke. This attack was not normal play. This was not a normal touch between an adult and a child. This was no accident, either. This was an adult man getting enjoyment at the expense of his young grandson coloring at his feet. This house was not safe.

The persistent memory of Papaw's action that day was the catalyst that revealed I had been touched in other inappropriate ways before that day. Papaw was too familiar and comfortable in this moment to stick his finger where "the sun don't shine"—this private place meant to be protected from unwanted intrusion.

How helpless I felt. I had been taken advantage of.

Someone in my family took away childhood innocence and laughed at his triumph.

The little boy who was his victim became a man who always wondered who would be next to stick their finger in his ass uninvited. I couldn't let my guard down. That humiliation became very comfortable to me. The shame of that moment is never far from the surface, engrained in my idea of self. It is projected to the world, while at the same time, I perpetually watch my back, or backside.

Looking at it now, I realize how deep the pain and hurt of that moment was. Fifty years later it still makes me weep. I was abused, and that abuse started years before that public moment. That act was bold, and Papaw felt confident no one would care.

No one cared. That was and still is astounding.

"Leave him alone," my mom did say, but what power was in those words? She let me go to live there just a few years later. I'm not sure if there was ever anyone who suspected Papaw's abusive behavior. As far as I know, Mamaw never said anything. As long as I was near, she got the emotional connection with me she needed, whatever the circumstances. Dad, just never said much about anything, locked in the prison of his own childhood with a father who beat him down, literally.

I now know that this one moment changed everything. It brought out in the open, even if it did take five decades to complete, the abuse that I had endured and would endure for a few more years. It revealed who Papaw was. It showed everyone else that he could not be trusted. Papaw got to continue to be a major part of my life until his death. I slept with him in his bed for years until I was a late teen and young adult. I was thrown to the wolves.

The memory of this event set me up for struggles that still are with me today. I often start with an expectation that others, whoever they may be, will stick it to me. Then, I guard myself against that with all of my energy, withholding complete openness. People in my orbit have to prove that they are not going to take advantage of or abuse me. I also am aware that, at any time, even when doing something that seems very basic like coloring a picture, I may be frightened to the point of jumping out of my skin with an unexpected and inappropriately placed action. I don't like to be the victim, no one does, but I expect that everyone wants to make me one.

It was an idyllic pastoral scene at my grandparent's house that day. Farmland stretching out in every direction, the sun shining through the door and windows warming the world. But, I was duped. Winter hadn't run away. He sat in his brown rocker waiting for just the right moment to "zip" it to me, when I least expected it, maybe even while other people were around. They wouldn't be of any help. I was alone in this, a blank picture other people want to fill in with their own color.

Another snapshot that stuck itself into my consciousness as an adult who had begun to realize that his childhood memories may not be so innocent is my earliest memory, which is of a woman's vagina. Actually, it is a woman's pubic hair and her vagina. The snapshot is as clear as if I were looking at a photo placed in an old-fashioned album. There is nothing else in the picture except for the few inches above, between her pubic area and belly button, and the few inches below, between there and her thighs.

I have had this picture in my mind for as long as I can remember. It isn't like it hangs out in my consciousness every moment, but it pops up on occasion, and as quickly as it comes, it goes away. I once assumed it was my mother. The story that unfolded around this frozen scene was that she was in the shower, and I, like many children, innocently entered the bathroom and pulled back the shower curtain. That was what I told myself for years. That was what I believed, but I gradually became less sure that was the entire story behind this mystery pubis.

This memory comes from the time just as my family, Mom and Dad and me, awaited the arrival of a sibling. My mom was pregnant. I was around three years old.

I knew where we lived at the time this memory was formed. It was on Moller Road on the south side of Columbus, Ohio. Like many others who had migrated north from southeast Ohio, my family had settled here after my parents married. I remember a good bit about the house. I have that ability. Things stay with me for years on end as snapshots in time, like a picture snapped and filed away. Another contributing factor is that, like most places, we didn't live there long. I mark time by the houses we lived in and the schools I went to. My parents moved every couple of years. I'm not sure why we moved so often. I went to seven schools from kindergarten through high school graduation. I lived in nine places during those same years. So, I knew the house.

I decided to take to the internet to satisfy my new desire to learn more. I looked for Moller Road on Google maps and scrolled through every curve on street view searching for a house that matched my memory of the outside and pictures I had seen.

During my virtual stroll, I finally came upon the split level with the garage on the right and the masonry flower planters lining the walkway from the driveway to the front door. The surrounding houses and yard were different than I remembered. It didn't look as nice as the pictures I had seen in actual photo albums. Then again, I hadn't laid eyes on this house for half a century. Still, it was the house.

What was I trying to find? Anything that would trigger more memory.

Our backyard was separated from the neighbor's yard by a fence. My mom and our neighbor would visit over the fence regularly. She and her husband watched me when my mom would need to be someplace else. The back fence became the drop off point for the handoff. Mom mentioned to this neighbor that she was looking for a new regular sitter to watch me and my sister full-time while she worked. My dad worked in construction. My Mom was a keypunch operator when data for computers had to be typed in code onto cards for entry. The neighbor was unable to watch us, but she said her older sister might be interested, and she was.

My mom said I never wanted to stay there with this sister. I cried every day. Mom would stress during work worrying and wondering how to keep from leaving us with her.

I could remember that the sitter would put me in a bedroom to take a nap, which I never did. I never wanted to. I would lay there, eyes open, listening. There was a grate in the floor. She lived in an older house where the second floor was heated by open grates in the floor that allowed heat from the first floor to float upward. I would hear men's voices from below. I often got out of bed to listen and watch through the grate, like a spy secretly gathering information and storing it away. It became a kind of game. Who would want to sleep in the middle of the day when you could do this? One day the men looked up just as I was looking down. I saw one of their eyes! I jumped back as quietly as I could onto the bed. Later, my mom would tell me this woman had two sons.

Twelve

LIFE WITH MAMAW AND PAPAW

Summer was my favorite time of the year growing up. Truth be told, it is still my favorite time of the year. I spent a majority of my summertime at Mamaw and Papaw's farm, which consisted of 60 acres between two ridges of hills in southeast Appalachian Ohio, just about a mile outside the town of Beaver. To my child's perspective, it was a beautiful spot. The house sat back from the main road, enough to have plenty of front lawn. There were buildings that sat away and behind the house that were intended for various uses but that were mostly obsolete by then—an old chicken coop, an outhouse, and a milk house that had once been used to store milk in a cool water pool in the floor. Long before my memory, the floor had been boarded over so that the building could be used like all the others, well, except for the outhouse, for storage. The outhouse wasn't used for storage or its intended purpose any longer, replaced by the indoor bathroom.

I played in the milk house after taking it back from the spiders and wasps who had claimed it over years of neglect. It became a place where I would spend hours. It was set up like a playhouse, with stuffed animal family members and friends. There was what we called a dish safe in the milk house. It was covered in cracked white paint. It sat majestically like an elderly witness to the past, curved legs, glass door front. I cleaned it out so it could hold my toys and items I would need for keeping house in this frontier of a building.

The milk house, like most every building surrounding the yard, was gray, weathered, and not painted. In today's world some woodworker would love to have this wood and reclaim it for new purposes. Then, it was just wood enclosing discarded items to hide away or maybe some garden tools.

There was also a block building containing a cellar and a second floor with an outside entrance in the back. Stairs, crumbling from having been trod upon by many feet over many years, led to the entrance on a second story. It was only a couple steps from the ground level to the concrete floor of that cellar, but in the heat of summer, the coolness was striking. It was like entering another world. It was an irresistible cobwebby, dark, damp, and dusty place. To the right were shelves from floor to low ceiling filled with home canned jars of green beans, beets, pickles, sauerkraut, and apples, pickled corn, and jelly, all harvested from the efforts in the garden.

That garden sat to the east of the house on a huge plot of ground. There was always the garden, no matter what. I loved the garden. It was amazing to me that seeds, or small starter plants, could be placed in the ground and produce food. Lots of food. Delicious food. I am talking about seriously amazing tomatoes. Now, we call them heirloom. Back then, they were just tomatoes. Grown from seed, passed down through generations year after year, which Mamaw meticulously saved and kept through the winter. Unlike the hybrid and genetically modified impostors we buy now, these genuine tomatoes were perfectly noiseless when they were cut with the knife. There was only juicy deliciousness.

There were rows of green beans. Green beans on bushes. Green beans on vines. Green beans that grew in the corn, right up the stalks. There was lettuce, cucumbers, corn, and sweet potatoes. There was what my grandmother called "arsh potatoes." I finally figured out that in her Kentucky accent she was saying Irish potatoes. I suppose it was some reference to the Irish potato famine, but I don't know. I accepted the term knowing Mamaw meant the potatoes that weren't sweet potatoes and left it at that. There was cabbage, green onions, carrots, beets, green peppers, and sometimes watermelon. All in meticulous, straight rows. My grandparents kept a beautiful garden that was completely weed-free. They were up before I ever thought of rising to work in the garden before the heat of the day. Mamaw, with her home-made bonnet, bent over the rows, old fashioned hoe in hand. That hoe had been worn down with the years of strong hands working ground growing food.

There was also a dog tied up to another building. He stayed there always. Only on a rare occasion do I ever remember anyone letting him off his chain to run. "Don't pet that dog. He'll bite you," was always the caution given to me by both grandparents with such seriousness and frequency that I was very afraid of the aptly named Nip. Nip was kind of short. He had black fur. I have no idea what breed he was. He likely had no noble pedigree, at least, he didn't look like it.

The story was that Nip was a dog my mom and dad had once. They couldn't keep him, and he ended up in his current living arrangements. It was as if he were confined to a prison for someone else's mistake. He seemed lonely. Because he was alone so much of the time, he wasn't socialized and was awkward around people. It wasn't like anyone gave him any attention. After all, I was warned against it for fear of injury. His exuberance combined with his isolation caused him to be one needy boy. Man, did he try and try to get noticed when someone was around. He would strain at his chain and bark and bark. I offered to pet him sometimes. I wanted to with everything in me, but mostly I resisted. Since I was taught to fear him, I did. I thought he would bite me. And, if he did, I'd get rabies. Or, at least, I'd have to have shots in my stomach like my mom, and the whole family, when she was a girl. To reinforce my fear of Nip, I had been told the story several times of another family dog who had bit someone years ago requiring everyone to be treated for rabies in case the dog was infected.

Nip's existence and entire world was bound up in a ten-foot radius of dirt and grass. He ate only the scraps from the meals Mamaw cooked. Those scraps would accumulate throughout each day, scraped into an old aluminum cooking pot with a handle. The pan's contents were dropped on the ground as an offering to appease his aloneness. Once in a great while, I got to do the dinner offering ritual before the pre-rabid beast. That was always fun. It allowed me to feel the tension in a dangerous moment. I would carefully get only so close, then dump the food and jump back, surprised that I lived to tell this tale another time.

My grandparent's house was on a country road. It was well-traveled, but neighbors weren't very close. You could see the neighboring houses, but there were fields several acres wide between. No one lived across the road in either direction for a quarter of a mile. An old barn that was graying from weather and lack of paint and that had a fading "Chew

Mailpouch Tobacco" sign, painted many years before my time. It sat nearly directly across the road from the house. I was told the barn wasn't a safe place. Occasionally, I would be allowed to go with someone who was making a trip across the road through the rusty gate into the barn lot and the barn itself. What a treat. You could see the daylight peeking through the boards making up the walls. Inside was empty and tall. Its only use was drying tobacco that was hung from the rafters.

My grandfather rented out a small plot of ground behind the house for growing tobacco and the fields across the street for grazing cattle or growing other crops, corn, soybeans, and wheat depending on the year. Always rented out. By the time I entered the family picture, Papaw and Mamaw didn't do any of the work. I remember the harvesting vividly. Big machines made their way across the fields. It was all so methodical and precise. Clouds of dust billowed upward behind the machinery. The rows were pristine.

Along with all other usual and expected farm activity, growing tobacco eventually stopped as well. I guess no one was interested, or the money wasn't so great. Growing tobacco is labor intensive. One year, my parents decided to take the job on themselves in order to make a little extra money, which they always seemed to need. That meant I got the opportunity to help. We hand planted rows and rows of tobacco plants with an archaic, although effective, gadget. It was a metal funnel with levers on the handle. The funnel held a plant on one side and was divided to hold water on the other. The operator pushed the funnel end in the plowed row, pulled the lever, and a plant dropped in the ground and the water came out in just the right amount to get the seedling plant off to a good start.

The farm also ascended up wooded hills in the back of the house. A thick growth of trees covered the upward sloping ground. Only rarely did we ever go there. A few times when my parents would be visiting, my dad would let Nip off the chain, and we would all take a walk in the woods. It fascinated me to have the dangerous, dreaded dog I was taught to fear walking around with us, sniffing at the world he could only imagine in his confinement, behaving himself.

Everything looked like a peaceful diorama. Looking down on the house, the farm, and the fields, and a few neighbors below, I could imagine in the light of day from this vantage point everything was sure to be perfect and happy. I was not an outdoor, walk-in-the-woods kid. As an adult, I enjoy nature most from my patio, but I did enjoy these moments with my parents and Nip. Nip running free at last seemed to bring a sense of adventure to the entire experience. It was as if we could all run free and off-leash to experience life from a more hopeful view.

Summer nights were a different story. Summer nights could be spooky. Those woods were the main culprits. Mamaw and Papaw had a window air conditioner in the kitchen and dining area, but they rarely turned it on. The night air was cool, so they thought. So, they opted for a couple of open doors with screens. I would have loved the comfort that I had at home in the city with central air conditioning, but that was rarely ever to be while I was at Mamaw's. They left the doors open at night revealing the utter enveloping darkness just on the other side of the screen. Some nights, I would peer out into the same darkness that held fears of Bigfoot and other creatures that I learned about on television shows like "In Search Of" and "Night Stalker."

One night, the darkness hid the source of a terrifying

sound. To this five-year-old, it sounded like a woman screaming—a piercing shriek as if she had been startled from behind. One thing was for sure. It came from the woods. For a moment, even though afraid, I pressed my face against the metal screen. I tried to see anything I could make out in the back of the house. Where did that sound come from? How close was it? Who was next? Afraid and yet curious like the person in a horror movie opening the creaky door—that was me in those moments.

"What was that?" I asked my grandparents. There were two explanations offered. My grandparents told me it was a she-fox. I assumed they meant a female fox, although I never did make sure. I just accepted that was right. The other explanation was the one I feared even more. It was more pervasive and altered my world and got personal. My Papaw answered, "That's Bucky getting someone in the woods." After hearing that explanation, I knew I would just stay in the light of the living room and away from that door in the summer kitchen.

Papaw was the custodian at the new high school just down the road. During summer months, he would take me with him to the school, big, empty, exciting, and scary without students or teachers. Chairs were stacked on top of the desks, so the floors could be polished, cleaned up after the nine months of students walking, dancing, running, and sliding all over them.

One place inside the school was always locked. I can still smell the Formaldehyde used for preserving specimens in the biology lab. The lab was a curiosity. I had never seen anything like it before. In it was a human skeleton suspended on a pole, likely used for learning bones and how they work. His name was Bucky. I hated Bucky, even if I was a little intrigued by him. He hung around in a dark locked lab. When I would go with Papaw on these summer days, he would chase me with Bucky, which scared me to death! I would scream. Still, I would want to see him the next time.

Bucky lived a dual life. Apparently, Bucky "got" bad kids. "Be good or Bucky will get ya," Mamaw and Papaw would say. Like horror movies I watched every Friday night on "Chiller Theater," I knew skeletons could show up anywhere. They could pass through barriers like walls, doors, and time itself. They could ascend out of vats of acid like the old black and white Vincent Price movie, "The House on Haunted Hill." I heeded the warning.

Mamaw's entire house had three bedrooms. One Mamaw's, one Papaw's, and one spare. I had never known a time when Mamaw and Papaw slept together. There was also a front room and a kitchen, but there was no hallway, just rooms connected to each other. You entered from the garage into a bedroom and then into the kitchen. There was one bathroom, which was connected to Mamaw's bedroom. In this bathroom was a closet. It was stuffed full of clothes and other items time had forgotten, pushed to the back wall and crowded so that many pieces of clothing, fancy dresses even, had fallen on the floor. The shelf above the closet rod was also jammed full. I would open the door to that closet with the same fear that I entered the science lab. It was dark. Once, I took a flashlight so I could see all the way to the back. Oh, how I was terrified of what might be staring back as I opened the creaky door and the light made visible the dark corners of this repository of history. Relief settled in when all I saw was the walls, dresses, hats, shoes, and shirts. The closet was where Bucky would lurk and hide to "get" me, according to those two trusted adults, Mamaw and Papaw, and I believed them.

Maybe he was just out stalking someone else right now, or perhaps he was waiting until darkness came outside.

I would sit on the toilet in the bathroom at night, alone, of course, and I would feel terribly nervous. What if he got me now? Bucky could just open the creaky door, and I was done. I was in no position to run away. Besides, the closet door, like the grip this place and these two people had on me, was between me and the only way out.

Thirteen

SOMEONE ELSE'S TERMS

Even though there were good times, it wasn't until years later that I realized how destructive Mamaw and Papaw were to me. They drove wedges between me and my mother. Mamaw always talked of my mom in negative ways and always spoke of my dad in positive ones. "Ann is lucky to have Lee Lykins." No one ever said he was lucky to have her, though.

Each summer, when the start of school neared, Mamaw had a yard sale. She told me it was so she could afford to buy my school clothes. She let me know that she had to provide my wardrobe, since my parents would only be sure that my sister had new clothes for school. They will see to that. There is no worry about that. I was set up. More than once Mamaw forced me to choose living with her and Papaw (although I'm certain she was more concerned about herself) over a life with Mom and Dad. I was placed in a situation that a boy should not have to be in. I guess I had a lot in common with Nip— living a life of connection but on someone else's terms. Years later I would discover that my life became chained to this place and these two adults in ways I didn't fully realize when

I was a boy, although there were hints.

During this time, I lived with my grandparents, and Mom and Dad would come to visit for the weekend. They would arrive on Friday night, stop in to drop off their luggage and then leave to go visit with my dad's family. Dad came from a family of seven siblings, most of whom still lived around the same area of southeast Ohio. On those Friday nights, Mom and Dad didn't arrive back to Beaver until after I had gone to bed, even after watching a horror movie at 11:30. The next day, they would eat breakfast with us and then be off again to visit my dad's family.

Still, I anticipated their visits with excitement. I would get to see them and our pet chihuahua, Duke. I romanticized their lives in the big city. On Sunday afternoons, when my parents would be leaving to go home to Columbus, I wanted to go with them. I wanted my parents to want to take me home. That's how I saw it as an eight year old. On the other hand, I wanted to be at Mamaw's house. It was fun to be at Mamaw's house. I could do about anything, as long as Mamaw remained the center of my world. I played with my cousin Sandy who had been born only two months before me. She lived with her parents and near her grandparents, just down the road. We loved to play outside and watch television and laugh. We could imagine nearly anything. The hills in Sandy's backyard would become the landscape of distant planets in faraway galaxies we explored.

The porch swing under the tree in her side yard became a taxicab or the bridge of the Starship Enterprise. The creek that ran across the back of the property, with a bridge over it in one location, was exotic. We crossed it and felt like we were in another world. Rolling hills bore the imprints of ancient glaciers creating ridges that became giant monster footprints for us.

I watched television at Mamaw's house. Shows like the Price is Right, Dark Shadows, General Hospital, Guiding Light, Carol Burnet, and Family Feud were staples. I played with games, puzzles, and the occasional doll. There was no limit to what I could imagine and the worlds I would make up, worlds into which I would immerse myself and take on the characters nearly 24/7. It all seems idyllic, like stuff written about in a "Highlights" or "Boy's Life" magazine. That was, unless you wanted to leave and escape up north like Mom had done nine years before.

There was this tension inside my young self. Sunday evening would come, and my parents would load their things in their 1969 silver Chevelle. It was a cool, two-door coupe with a black vinyl top. There was an eight-track player that played clear beautiful sounds of songs from Creedence Clearwater, Steppenwolf, Johnny Cash, and even Lynn Anderson. The eight tracks were kept in a large black faux snakeskin case that was lined with red velvet in the back-seat floorboard. It was large enough that whoever sat where it was had to rest their feet on its top. Mom and Dad would begin saying goodbyes and getting in the car, and I would vacillate. Stay or go. My parents would take me if I wanted. No one ever made a case for it though. It was up to me at these Sunday evening moments. More than once I got in the car. It was clear Mamaw did not want me to go. My parents didn't beg me to go with them, but she would beg me to stay. As we drove away and the car headed down the country road, looking back through the car rear window, I would see Mamaw crying.

On one particular Sunday, I had been at Mamaw's house for three weeks. Mom and Dad, having been to Mamaw's for a weekend visit, were packing to leave to get back before work the next day. The traffic would be rough with all the people doing the very same thing. Route 23 carried many migrants from Columbus back and forth to home in the southern part of the state, or even Kentucky, or West Virginia. The suitcases were loaded into the car along with canned goods from that summer's garden. As they packed, I became very sad that they were leaving, and I was not going with them.

"Can I go home?" I asked Mom, which started a conversation about whether I would stay home this time. Mom was skeptical, unsure of what was going to follow if she tried to take me from the matriarch. I assured her with all my eight years of life experience that I would stay in Columbus this time. I wanted to see my sister and Duke. I missed them. I was a child who had his head, heart, and life in two places. One was in the hills of southeast Ohio, and the other was in the city. Mamaw's beds were always comfortable, but I missed having my own room. So, I packed up too. I was going to go home, and I was going to stay there. This time would be the time. This one was different. It would be fun. I belonged with Mom, Dad, and Ruth, right? We were a family.

As I went to get in the car, Mamaw begged me to stay. "Don't go," she manipulated, a noticeable frown on her face. She cried (or acted like it, I'm not sure I could tell the difference). She tried all the tricks in her possession. Facial expressions of sadness. Voice inflections to communicate hurt. Wiping of tears.

I made my way to the back seat. This was the time before kids had to be restrained in car seats or boosters or even a seatbelt. I perched myself between the two front seats and the middle console. That way, I could see out the front windshield. I watched through the front window as Mamaw wiped her face.

Finally, we pulled out of the gravel driveway and onto the road. We may have broken free of the driveway and started our journey home, but I was in turmoil in that back seat. Inside me was the pull, strengthened by the image of Mamaw. My heart was confused. Inside was the memory of her house. Inside were feelings of longing for home and my family and Mamaw and Papaw and Sandy and this southern offshoot of my family. And, there was the image of Mamaw. Crying. I had hurt her. She was sad. How could I do that to her?

I cried and cried and through my tears intensely demanded that I be taken back after making it just five miles down the road. It was not going to be different than the other times. I wasn't going to leave Mamaw in her pain. No matter what I needed or what might have been best for me, Mamaw was in control, and her gravitational pull was stronger than any sun in the universe, and I was pulled back. I could not do it. I would go back, and all would be well. Mamaw would be all right. The situation I had created would be fixed.

Dad turned the car around and made his way back down the road toward the modest white house and the gravel driveway that was waiting to accept me back. Even though I was supposed to be headed north, it was a quick little excursion, a jaunt of futility. Very few people could escape Mamaw's influence, Mom included. It was best to not try. I got out of the car and Mamaw, in the house, was ecstatic to see me when I burst through the door, as if she didn't know this would be the outcome. Mom and Dad left again. I was welcomed home like the prodigal from the distant country.

It took me 48 years to discover that this moment, and the other thwarted attempts to go home, set me up for a life of feeling responsibility for everyone else's feelings. In a counselor's office at the age of 56, I had an epiphany that I felt responsible for everyone and everything. I had spent my life trying to control what happened around me so that everything stayed calm and in place. I didn't want anyone upset with me. Along with that came the realization that I had believed that, if anyone was upset, it was likely at me and was my fault. Therefore, I had to do something about it until the situation was reset to some sense of normal. Normal for me was defined as the absence of conflict. No one was upset. All was humming along and leaving me alone. Even when there was conflict, and certainly over the years as a leader, my decisions resulted in conflict. During those times, it was really difficult for me to be at ease without obsessing nearly constantly about the upset people until some situation came along to change the dynamic.

In the counselor's office with my wife, Shelly, beside me, I realized that the difficult time she was discussing was not my fault. I could do nothing about it. I could only support her and be present. She had to endure it. Only she could grow from the circumstance by going through it. That was it. I could not fix it. That really pissed me off. It made me very uncomfortable. For once, the first time, I was just sitting back without controlling a situation so it would get back to normal (based on my definition).

No matter how many times over the years in my mind I see Mamaw standing at the driveway crying while begging me to stay with her, in a manipulative tone of voice, I thought I was responsible for her. I projected her onto every other person in the world. I experience Mamaw in the driveway when a parishioner threatens to leave the church if we don't sing more patriotic hymns on civil holidays. I see Mamaw in the driveway every time my wife cries. I see Mamaw in the driveway when I tell someone no. I see her in their look—a look I am sure means they are upset, and if upset, it must be with me since I am responsible for the universe.

The tug-of-war that went on in my eight-year-old self that day repeats with frequency. It is just part of who I am now, and I didn't even realize it until that gifted counselor said, "We know where your feeling of responsibility and control comes from." I wanted to dig around and discover the source of it. As soon as she said that, I knew in the deepest part of myself where it came from too. Mamaw in the driveway. Mamaw who pulled me back to fix her situation. Mamaw who pulled me back to fulfill her needs. Mamaw who cried because I had made her upset. I was set up for a life of impossible expectation.

I finally learned, though, that I am not responsible. I am not able to fix anyone. I can't control a damn thing. Some things, most things, just are. Sometimes those things we face are just hard. They make us cry. They make us mad. They make us sad. And, they have nothing to do with me. I can listen. I can hold people. I can give comfort. I can show up to be present and offer support. I can empathize. No matter how much others and my old self may blame me, most often it's their own shit.

That day in the car with my parents was a perfect image of my entire life spent sitting in the middle of the backseat looking out the front window waiting for the reaction to my decisions. I was placed in the middle of a struggle between adults who put themselves above my best interest. My parents may have thought being with this woman was best for me, giving me stability that they couldn't guarantee with their work. When I was with them, I was bounced around to sitters and school. Wasn't this better?

Thirty-five years later, in a counselor's office, I would finally bring to light what I always knew. More than love for me, Mamaw was using me to get what she didn't have. A child to raise. I won't go as far as to say a child to love because what I experienced wasn't love as much as selfishness. It wasn't about what was best for me. Like the dog tied up in the back, I was fed scraps of what passed as love to appease my entrapment. Fear was my chain. I was placed in the middle trying to please everyone in the situation, and it stuck. Living in the middle became a life pattern.

I've seen Mamaw's face in many faces since that day. The Mamaw in the driveway has taken many forms desperately trying to pull me in to her orbit as she sucks the life out of me to give meaning to hers. The difference now is that I keep going, heading north toward home, breaking free from the gravitational pull of a weeping Mamaw—breaking free like a rocket that finally breaks out of the earth's force that wants to hold on to it as long as possible.

Fourteen

HIDING REALITY

I slept with Papaw most nights, but I did sleep with Mamaw some too. It seems like we had a pattern of trading off nights, but I don't remember the details of the schedule. This went on until I was in Junior High School. I always liked sleeping in Mamaw's bedroom. I think it has something to do with the truth that raised to the top of my consciousness seven years ago.

In Papaw's room, which was adjoined to Mamaw's by a door, the double bed Papaw and I shared stood in a corner. I slept on the side of the bed next to the window. Papaw slept on the side of the bed next to the door that led to the garage. In the corner near the other two doors—one leading to Mamaw's room and the other out into the kitchen—was a portable record player. I used that record player a lot. I collected singles or 45 rpm records, although at the time I didn't call it collecting. I just enjoyed buying the single hit songs, usually for one dollar, whenever I had any money. "Billy Don't Be A Hero" by Bo Donaldson and the Heywoods was one of the first purchases. "Seasons in the Sun," by Terry Jacks and "Black and White" by Three Dog Night were others among my growing collection. I still collect these records and have over 200 now.

I didn't buy very many long play albums ever. I stuck to spending my money on the songs I liked and not gambling on other songs I may not know. One I listened to often was a record of Grimm's Fairy Tales being read by different voices acting out the characters. There was another that was a Disney version of the "Three Little Pigs." Before getting in bed when I slept with Papaw, I would put one of those two records on the turntable and let them play as I went to sleep. Since the record player shut off on its own, I always hoped to be asleep by the time the voices told the last story, but it never happened. I listened to every story to the end of the side being played. Every night, the same stories. I would choose side A or B based on whether I wanted to hear the fisherman's wife nag at him to use up his wishes to make her wealthy and happy—"Throw me back. Throw me back into the ocean," the flounder begged every time to no avail. The wife ends up a fish in the end—or Rumpelstiltskin spinning his straw to gold in kind of a bond-servant situation. They were dark stories with troublesome endings. Not Disney material for sure. Nonetheless, I played them religiously trying to get to sleep.

Sleeping with Papaw was no happy fairy tale either. I remember hearing him peeing in a can he kept by the bed. It was a big can, like for Crisco or lard, with the label removed. It was rusty from being used for such a reason for too long. Due to prostate trouble that he would discover in later years, he had to urinate in the middle of the night with some frequency. Mamaw didn't want him to wake her up by coming through her room to get to the bathroom. Besides, my child's mind figured, who would want to go in there at night when it's dark and the whole house is asleep? That's a great time for Bucky the skeleton to pounce! But, that was my story to fear. I guess Papaw's story to fear may have been Mamaw. No one ever talked about why they had separate rooms. Only once do I ever remember them kissing or being affectionate. On their 50th wedding anniversary, Mamaw opened a gift from Papaw. It was a new gold wedding band. My mom had actually picked it out and wrapped it. After carefully unwrapping the small package, Mamaw chased a grinning Papaw kissing his cheek with a peck. That was a first, last, and only act of affection I witnessed.

My mom occasionally speculated through the years as to why they never had children, beyond the obvious family relation thing. No one knew. People weren't all that open to talking about such things. Mom asked other family members. If they knew, no one ever said. Once in a while, I would be told by Mamaw of young folks who would stay with them. Some they practically raised, a lot like they were doing with me. All of them were boys. It seems like a nice story of willingness to help a person or family in need at first glance. Now I am not at all convinced. Mamaw had a need to have a child to call her own. Papaw had other needs.

When I was 54 years old, in the counselor's office, sitting with my eyes shut listening to music and waves rolling from ear to ear through the headset I was wearing, I started to cry. There was something about playing these records at night that was off, not an innocent memory. As we were working through the memory, I tensed. Clearly, in my mind's eye, I could see that Papaw was jerking off. His sounds, although quiet, spun through the darkness. I lay next to him. I was trying to get to sleep. I didn't want to listen. I didn't even quite understand what was happening.

"I want to be the richest woman in the world," the Fisherman's wife said from the record player in the corner of the room. And, cha-ching, the sound of a cash register was heard. Crowd noises could be heard, like at a mall. Wall Street sounds, masking what I didn't want to hear coming from the other side of the bed. Some nights, Papaw included me in his sexual activities, touching me in ways that no Papaw should touch a little boy. In the counselor's office I was angry. "How could you do that to me?" I said to Papaw in the moment in my mind. The sounds of the Flounder from Grimm's Fairy Tales, "Throw me back into the ocean!" could not hide the truth any longer. These stories played each night to hide the sounds of what I couldn't bear to hear or think about. The sounds of a man and a frightened boy came roaring to the present moment from nearly 50 years before.

Fifteen

BUILT ON LIES

Throughout my life, especially when I was a teen and early adult, Mamaw showered material things on me. She did this much more than she did toward my sister. I may never know why, but for some reason I was the object of her devotion and loyalty. She gave me anything and everything I wanted. Literally. As a kid, I would just ask Mamaw for the toy I wanted, and I would have it. As a teenager, after I learned to drive, I would make trips to Mamaw's house, but not because I wanted to see her. I would go when I was low on money. By that time, I had my own bedroom in her house, and in that room was a small cedar chest that sat on a dresser. I knew that inside would be a wad of cash. I never knew how much would be there, but it always had something. It was our secret. She said so. She told me to check it every time I visited. There were times I felt guilty that my sister didn't get this same treatment, but I would suppress those feelings. I was hooked like a drug addict who needed his next fix.

When I was in college, there was a coat I wanted. I was working a job at the time, so I could have bought it, eventually. The price was more than I could pay in the moment, so I put it on lay-away. I told Mamaw about it, and as expected, I got the cash to get it out of lay-away so I would have something warm to wear while walking around campus. I already had a coat that was plenty warm. I just wanted the other one. That was the way it went. Always.

As I look back on that reality now, I believe she kept me in her circle of influence by doing this. I feel like I was manipulated. Like her love, my love, was based on a transaction. It worked. Mamaw was supreme in my life and my identity.

I think Mamaw felt threatened by other people who were in my life. She saw other relationships as competition with her. Whenever I was on the phone with a friend, she would beg me to get off. If I wanted to visit a friend, she would make me feel guilty. Once at 16 I was driving two friends to a movie in a nearby town. We were going to Wheelersburg to watch "Return of The Jedi." That entire day, Mamaw and Papaw attempted to appeal to my moral compass. They tried everything to get me to call off this fool-hearty trip. They even said that watching movies was idol worship, to which my friend Sandy said, "If he falls on the floor in the cinema and starts worshiping an idol, I'll drag him out."

This sort of thing happened even with me and my own parents. A few times when Mom and Dad were ready to leave Mamaw's house to make the trip back north to Columbus, I grabbed onto my mom's legs, near her ankles. I held her legs and cried and yelled for her not to go and not to leave me. I always stayed. Mom didn't take me with her, and I didn't ever have the courage to make the break. I learned well.

At least once a year or so as a kid, I was sick. When I was about five, I remember getting my nauseated self to the bathroom to sit or kneel, but miserable either way. I cried and begged to go to Mamaw and Papaw's house. I wanted to see Mamaw. My Mom called and told them what was happening. Just for me, Mamaw had Papaw drive her to Columbus. She never learned to drive. She even paid Papaw gas money to take her places. At about 10:30 at night, I was bundled up in their car, nauseated, and cold, sitting between them both in the front seat where Mamaw could comfort me and hold me. I settled down into the comfort of what I knew. A soothing codependence. We drove the hour and a half back to Beaver.

Clearly, the abuse comes into this entire mess of emotion and behavior. It isn't so easily untangled—the need to keep me quiet, the need to keep me dependent, the unhealthy need for Mamaw to have a child, the need she had for someone to love her. All of that, and likely more I don't even know or understand, became the cords that held me in this trap. On the one side was a manipulative couple of elders who took advantage of me for physical and emotional pleasure. On the other side were two young people who had a kid and didn't know what to do. That is not all of the story where my mom is concerned though.

PART FOUR

DAMNED

Sixteen

DECEIT

My mom was caught up in her own life. Her past trauma was greater than almost anything else in her life. When I came along, she was not ready to be a mother. I think she knew it, but getting married and having babies is what a young woman did, right? For sure, it is what a young woman who is desperate to escape the abuses of a strict, oppressive home does. A young woman, 17 year old girl really, coming out of high school, finding out her parents were not her biological parents might do that. She found out her mother was a vague acquaintance who had been relegated to the shadows. Her father was a person who had not been kind to her. She had thought he was her brother—a brother with kids of his own, raised as nieces and nephews to her, the lies piling up. The web that entangled all the players in this game of Twister (or Twisted!) was indeed woven with deceit. Deceit isn't a good foundation to build lives on. Once something begins to expose the untruths, the foundation cracks. Then, it all comes crashing down. And, it did.

So, here is this young woman, married and living 80 miles from where she grew up, with no way to know what to expect.

No one had told her. No one had helped her find who she was or what she wanted in life. No one had encouraged her to dream. No one had helped her maneuver life. "Marry him. His family has money," were the only words of wisdom and advice served up to her from her parents. Those same people who were really my great grandparents ended up, through more deceit and manipulation, involved in my life more than they should have been. Those were the same people who abused me in ways that no child should endure. They took from me innocence and my trust in myself and others. They tried to silence me like so many others before me so the secrets would stay secret.

Seventeen

SECRECY

My parents, Ann and Lee, were married when my mom was just graduating high school at 17 years old. My dad was 23. Dad managed a small grocery and what might be called a dry-goods store in Beaver, Ohio. The store was owned by my dad's father and was named Lykins Market.

The town of Beaver, Ohio, was and is small. The current population is about 450 people. At the time of my parent's courtship, it was closer to 350. So, not much has changed.

My mom grew up in Beaver. She was raised by Luster and Versa Jenkins. Luster and Versa were both from Magoffin County, Kentucky, and had come to Ohio, as many people from their family did, for work during World War II. They crossed the Ohio River and settled in Springfield, which is about two hours north of Beaver.

Luster had been married two other times. He had a son, Buford, whom he raised alone after Buford's mother died from illness. Versa, Luster's wife was his first cousin. I have no idea, and neither does anyone who would be willing to say, why the two got married. They never had children together.

Buford fathered a daughter with a woman named Eloise. I assume he fell in love with her even though they never married for reasons never spoken. All the details are unclear. Again, no one talked about it. Maybe no one knew the details. Maybe the only ones who knew are all dead now. Whatever the reason for the silence, it led to much struggle and pain in the lives caught in its grip.

Hiding the truth was a pattern in my family. There was a perpetual culture of silence and coverup.

When I was about ten years old, I was told that Versa and Luster were not Ann's parents. Buford and Eloise were. The way I heard it, Ann's biological mother, Eloise, was not caring for her. When they all lived in Springfield together, Versa would go to visit Eloise and Ann and find Ann dirty and in a state of neglect. It got to the point that Versa took Ann from Eloise when she came upon Ann dirty and naked playing in an empty bathtub during one of these visits.

Ann didn't know this truth until she was planning to marry Lee Lykins in 1962 and needed her parent to sign for permission. She was told this story. Buford was not her brother as she had been led to believe for 17 years. He was her father. Maybe this explained the anger that seemed to seep out of him on many occasions in the way he treated her.

Eloise had been present in Ann's life, visiting a few times, with Ann never really understanding who she was. But once the truth was out in the open, Eloise was seen as a threat. Eloise was never seen again after the bridal shower Ann invited her to.

Eloise's life was a mystery. Ann knew a few details that she gathered from those who would talk about it. Eloise had several other children after Ann. She also had several other men in her life after Buford. She stayed in Springfield, Ohio, where she raised her family. By the time I heard the story, Eloise was dead. She had been shot dead by a jealous man who had found her in the arms of another.

Years later, Ann set out to find some piece of her past that might help her discover answers to mysteries that left a gap in her memory and her soul. Ann knew enough detail to know that Eloise, her biological mother, was buried at a cemetery in Ray, nestled in the hills of rural Vinton County, Ohio.

Ann made the journey to Ray to find her mother's grave. Just as the road turned sharply, she came upon the small cemetery, grasses overgrown at its perimeter. As she walked in, the bright sunlight through the rows of those who had been laid to rest in a place that must have a home-like connection, she wondered why Eloise had ended up in Ray. Springfield was 80 miles away.

Ann did find her mom's grave that day. Eloise Click, 1926-1972. She decided she would leave a note on the tombstone. Maybe someone in the family would find it and would know about her connection to this woman's life, her first child, born from war-time love. Eloise, whose life was cut so short, really didn't know much about her now 48 year old daughter either.

The note she left read "From your first-born, Ann."

In the meantime, Eloise's other children, all adults by then, were searching for the lost sister they knew existed. A family member contacted an uncle who told them their oldest sister had been raised by Luster Jenkins. After finding his phone number, they called and asked about Ann. Adhering to the code of secrecy, Luster wouldn't tell them anything. A few days later, they called again, and that time he gave in and told them where Ann worked.

Ann received a call from her brother Butch and three

sisters. They made the trip to meet her for the first time only two days later. That's when she discovered there were 13 more brothers and sisters, all born after Ann. They had heard her story, but she never knew anything of theirs, or how she fit into it. She didn't even know there was another story that had been running parallel to her life for nearly half a century.

This discovery started a search for more answers to questions that Ann had never known to ask. Luster and Versa, who raised her, would never talk about anyone in that part of her family. Her aunts and uncles would not talk, save one, an aunt named Tennessee, Luster's sister. Tennie told her about grandparents and others and filled in the story as best she could. She didn't know all the details, of course, as she was younger than the others. However, no one else would tell Ann more of what completed her story and filled in the unspoken parts. The story was lost in the unspoken fear of truth, as if speaking reality would somehow alter the foundations that held the world together. I guess in some ways they would be altered. A narrative had been relied on to hold people in their places and give justification for connections that made up what was called family. It wasn't one or two people who wove this false narrative of deceit. It was many.

My parents, Lee and Ann, started their life together in the context of the uncovered truth that the people she had called Mom and Dad for 17 years were really her grandparents. On the verge of a new chapter in life, Ann was discovering she was not who she thought she was. The people in her life had been shuffled around to take on different roles. There was the brother, who was actually her father, parents who were actually her grandparents, and a family acquaintance who was her mother. Added to them, Ann moved to Columbus with her husband.

About eleven months later, in May of 1963, I was born into this story. Ann never really knew what to do with a baby. Let's face it, why would she? She was barely an adult, and that by age only. Her world turned upside down, and she was spiraling. I spent a lot of time at Mamaw and Papaw's house in Beaver from my earliest moments. I suppose that arrangement helped Mom.

Dad had kind of fallen into a career as a brick mason. Before he and Mom married, he decided he didn't want to manage a store any longer. He wanted a job where he could pack a lunch and go to work and go home at the end of the day. The first job he got when applying for other employment was as a masonry laborer. The laborer keeps the masons supplied with bricks, stone, or block. They also keep the mortar supply filled. They assist however needed to keep the skilled workers efficiently operating. For his work, Dad earned $1.50 per hour. His second job was with a relative who owned a construction company. Dad was still a laborer, but since it was a union job, his pay went to $3.00 per hour. While working there, the men on the job taught Dad to lay brick.

I've seen his masonry work throughout my life, and it is beautiful. A couple of times later on he even started his own masonry company. I've heard stories over the years of some of the funnier antics and strange requests from clients. One of my favorite stories was the client having Dad build a fireplace with white brick. The request was to use a variety of rainbow color tinted mortar between. Those colors were to be used a few inches at a time in the full course of bricks. Keeping the colors off the white brick and having to use a small amount of red and then switch to a small amount of blue, etc., was quite difficult. He said it was one of the ugliest fireplaces he ever saw, but he, no doubt, did an excellent job at it.

In the winters, Dad didn't make much money, since not much brick or block gets laid in the snow and cold. Mom had to work to help supplement Dad's salary. The tensions with Mom's own identity, her inexperience with relationships that were healthy, and the responsibility to care for a baby were too much at times. After Christmas in the second grade, I went to live in Beaver with Mamaw and Papaw. I lived with them from the middle of second grade until the end of third grade. It was the place I called home. I spent more time there than with my parents. The bus stopped in front of the white, aluminum siding clad, one-story house every school day morning to take me to Beaver Elementary School.

This very school was the same one my mom had attended. We had the same second grade teacher, Mrs. Lamb. She never seemed to like to be bothered by kids. At afternoon milk break, she would open her carton and place a straw in her mouth first and then put it slowly in the carton of milk. I came to understand later that Mrs. Lamb was what we would call a germaphobe today it also explained why she opened every doorknob with a brown paper towel from the wall dispenser in her classroom. She likely was in quite a state of distress when a girl, one afternoon following lunch of hot dogs and something with pineapple, threw up at her desk, which was right next to Mrs. Lamb's desk.

I learned later from my mom that me living with Mamaw and Papaw wasn't really abandonment by my parents. That was good to know, since I had spent time in counselor's offices trying to figure out why I felt abandoned, left, as if I had parents who didn't want to be bothered with children. They thought it was for my good, my mom told me in the car coming home for Christmas break during my freshman year of college. After all, Mom and Dad couldn't take care of me and work full time. In their minds, they couldn't provide a stable environment for me, or my sister, Ruth, who spent much of that time with the Stephens. I always thought that my mother, Ann, struggled with finding herself, knowing who she really was. She was married right out of high school and had a baby soon after. I still think it was hard for a young, inexperienced Ann to find herself tethered to the demands of motherhood. She was, in many ways, a child herself, just learning about life.

And there was Mamaw, Versa, the woman who had already taken Ann from her mother and raised her without formal adoption, hiding it all along. My Mom would tell me many years later that Mamaw pressured her to let her have me, and up to when I was in fourth grade, I lived with Mamaw more than with my parents. Mamaw had snatched my mother away from my actual grandmother, and when I came along, she wanted me. I'm sure this filled a need for some purpose in life for Mamaw. I would find out later that Mom wasn't the first to be taken in, taken care of, fed, and housed by Mamaw. To be sure, Mom was the only one Mamaw made such an all-in commitment to for the rest of her life, to the point of hiding the truth of my mother's lineage, which helped to keep everyone and the story under control.

So, I ended up, like my mom, in the influence of a woman who was married to her cousin and had no children of her own. I was in a place where I was both overwhelmed with connection that passed for love and the victim of the need to be loved that controlled everything and everyone it grasped.

So, I too found myself in Beaver, Ohio. It was another place I called home.

Eighteen

HUSH CHILD

One day, when I was about five years old, I was outside and said, "I hate you" to my mom who was inside the house. I thought Mom was out of earshot. She wasn't. Since it was summer, the main door was open, and the screen was little barrier to my anger reaching her ears.

I know kids say things like that, but I carried around an anger that was just underneath the surface only kept in place by the sun and rolling hills and play when I was in Beaver. That place and being with Mamaw and Papaw kept it pushed down until it burst forth in the most surprising times. I remember vividly screaming at the top of my lungs from my bedroom at my mom, "Fuck! I hate you!" I was ten. I didn't even know exactly what "fuck" meant. I was angry, and it just came out. I had heard Papaw say it only once. I don't even know if he was exactly angry when he said it. I had heard some kids say it, but otherwise that was a seldom used word in my family and even among friends.

The anger inside that young boy seems totally reasonable to me now. However, when I was ten years old and even younger, I didn't have an awareness of what was happening to me. I didn't have any way to explain it or process it. Things that were part of my life were just life. They were normal to me. As much as I have worked on these needs and issues in my life over the years, I still have to pay attention to the feeling that arises when I feel as if I am being dismissed. "Fuck it!" would still arise in me, as if I were standing in that bedroom on the east side of Columbus and my mom had set me off. "Fuck it!" I just recently gained an appreciation for that phrase. Other than that one time as an angry ten year old, I never ever used that word in my life, and I still don't say it out loud (well, not much), but it does have an attitude all its own. An attitude that has helped me on several occasions to express what I'm feeling.

These patterns continued as an adult for me. I have often felt as if I wasn't being heard, as if I had to struggle to get noticed. I feel like I have spent a lifetime saying, "Here I am. I am drowning. I am alone. No one cares. Can you hear me?!"

At one point during elementary school, we lived next to a family of five, a mom and dad and three kids, two brothers and a sister, close in age to me and my sister. We became friends with the kids. Our neighborhood was full of kids, and we hung out with several of the neighbors during the time we lived there. Even my parents had friends in the neighborhood. It was nice to be close to the people we shared a street with.

We also shared a basement with a neighbor who lived across the street from us. They were one of the few houses that had a basement on the entire street. During tornado warnings, which seemed to happen with frequency, many people gathered in their house, waiting for the all-clear. It was fun. There was good conversation and laughter in the midst of the possibility of shared destruction.

We walked to and from school then. No, it wasn't uphill both ways. It was just life. In the rain, we wore yellow plastic slicker raincoats and matching boots over our shoes. Many moms stayed home, and students would actually leave school and walk home for lunch. My mom worked outside of the home, so my sister and I walked to the neighbors' at lunch and before and after school. There were a couple of other neighborhood kids who were part of this impromptu after-school daycare. The neighbor mom was home all day and didn't drive, so she was a go-to babysitter.

One day when my sister and I were going over the events of our day, she told me about an experience she had while at the neighbors once without me. She witnessed as the mom of the family yelled at one of the sons and then pushed his head into the wall, apparently not hard, just a whack, but still it frightened my sister. We knew from being right next door in a neighborhood where the houses were not far apart that there were moments when that family was loud with their emotions and their discipline, and we had witnessed it on a few occasions. Even at our young age—I was in fifth grade at the time, my sister in second—we were uneasy.

The next day as I was walking to school with one of my friends from down the street, I told him about the incident relayed to me. We commented on how that was consistent with what we had seen and heard before. Later in the week, I was called into the neighbors' house, and there was the dad, mom, and my mom, and my friend in whom I had confided. Apparently, my friend had told someone else, and it had gotten back to one of the family and then to the mom and dad. They were horrified that I would have said such a thing to someone. There was a lot of guilt being laid down. "This could be terrible if others heard what you said." "I've never done anything like that." "We could get into trouble…" I told them that's what my sister said she saw. I don't know why she'd make it up.

I remember thinking, "That's what my sister saw, and I believe her, and yes, you have acted like that before."

My mom apologized for me and said, "I'll take care of this one."

After we walked inside our house next door, she spanked me with her clothes brush. I was sent to my room and was grounded to my room between school and dinner the rest of the week.

Even as a kid, I didn't quite get it. As an adult, that memory has been the subject of contemplation, reflection, and even some counseling sessions. I now understand it as one of several moments when I got punished for telling the truth. That day standing under the hot glare of my angry interrogators, I told the truth. They were lying, and what I said didn't matter. Not only did they not believe me, but the one who might have trusted her kids to not spread lies punished me. My sister escaped the punishment. I guess my sin was the bigger one, telling another person who told someone else. So, I learned that my truth, my opinion, what I observed or said, couldn't be trusted. It happened at least on one other time in our family history.

It was hot and humid in August of 1973 when my dad, mom, sister, and I piled in the silver gray 1969 Chevy Chevelle to head for Montana. We ate in the car, having packed food in a cooler. We slept all but one night in the car, stopping once to sleep in a rest area with doors locked. We set out on our adventure with none of the modern items we would now consider necessary for traveling that distance with a seven and ten year old. There were no tablets or cellphones with games to pass the hours. There were no onboard movies. There was no satellite radio or streaming service to play exactly the music we wanted. The Chevelle didn't even have air conditioning. There was just my dad, mom, me, my sister, and a selection of eight-track tapes. It seemed enough, most of the time.

We drove through the lake country of Minnesota, and the flatlands of North Dakota. Roosevelt National Park and the Painted Canyon of North Dakota were amazing sights. We had no GPS or internet to give us a hint of what we could see. We were just explorers with the windows down and the wind in our faces taking in what the world had to offer. We were surprised that Montana took us nearly an entire day to drive across. Libby, Montana, our final destination, was in the farthest northwest corner of the state. It was also a surprise to me that we spent the first day driving through flat country and not the mountains I expected. Eventually, the flat land gave way to jagged rocky crags of mountains in Glacier National Park. We drove through amazing landscapes around every turn. Snow in August! It lay on the mountaintops like powdered sugar on the tops of brownies.

We arrived at Uncle Roland's, my dad's brother, and were greeted by him, my aunt, and their two daughters. We saw these family members only occasionally when they made the trip to Ohio. They had left a few years before. I didn't know their story, still don't very well, the distance keeping us apart in body and memory. Two of Dad's seven siblings, a brother, Roland, and a sister, Dawn, had gone with their spouses to start a new life in this wild place made exotic by stories of mountain lions, bears, and fishing. I hadn't traveled further than my grandparent's home in Beaver, Ohio, from Columbus before this, so exotic was no far stretch.

We were staying with Roland and his family. We went

inner-tubing in a stream. I thought that was great fun until someone had to have a leech pulled off them. At that point, the wilderness was too real for me. We ate a whole salmon that had been prepared from a previous catch. There were conversations, play with cousins, television watching, and a trip to Fort Steele in Canada.

We had been sleeping and spending most of our time with Uncle Roland and his family, and they had been great hosts. I slept in a bedroom that was usually used as an office with a couch in one corner, comfy enough for a ten year old. There was a large picture window in the front of the house. Uncle Roland had a nice plush recliner that faced that window. Through it you could see the majestic mountains with their snow topped peaks. I had never seen anything like it. The trip opened my eyes to the beauty of the Earth and the West. I had fun getting to know my cousins who had lived these thousands of miles from the rest of us in Ohio.

After we had already been there several days, we were invited to dinner with Aunt Dawn and her family. Dawn had asked us over for dinner before, but this night my parents took her up on the offer. We left Roland's to drive the few miles to Dawn's house. It was early enough in the evening that the sun was still out in full force. My dad drove, of course, as he had the entire four days it took to drive through Ohio, Illinois, Wisconsin, and North Dakota. My mom sat up front. My sister and I sat in the back seat, patiently watching the block-patterned plowed ground go by the windows as we made our way across that great land. During the drive to dinner, my mom and dad discussed whether we were going to stay all night. Apparently, Dawn had mentioned the possibility. Dad and Mom were acting as if we would. They had brought some items in a suitcase in case.

Dawn and her husband and three children were excited to see us. Well, at least Dawn and Tim were. The kids were not sure about the strangers from Ohio, just as much as I wasn't sure about them. I am an introvert after all. None of this, even with family, came easily, but not for any particular reason. We just didn't know each other. Dinner was really good. We sat around a big table and shared food, laughter, and stories. After dinner, the adults caught up on the miles and years between them as the kids played outside until darkness crept in and we had to retreat to the inside. That was actually ok with me. I preferred the inside. Except for the beauty of the mountains that surrounded us, I didn't get all the attraction of bugs and heat that the great outdoors held. That view could be enjoyed from inside through a picture window. No need to go outdoors.

Not long after darkness enveloped the view of those mountains and the kids came inside joining the adults in the living room, Mom mentioned that it was time to go. Aunt Dawn was sad to see us go, saying they hadn't got to see us all that much. She then invited us all to stay the night. My parents were adamant that we all needed to get back and were unable to stay the night anyway. That confused and disappointed me. This was turning out to be like buying a Christmas tree. My parents were fickle. On separate occasions over many years, Mom would say at the dinner table, "We are going to get our tree tonight and decorate it." I would be ecstatic with excitement. It would consume all of my thoughts and energy. "When are we going to buy the Christmas tree?'

"Oh, we aren't doing that tonight. Another time," would come the devastating response to this boy who had his hopes dashed. It was hard to count on what was said at the moment of the saying. Anything promised may or may not happen.

Just because they said it, didn't make it true. The plan to stay the night had been discussed, but when it came right down to it, I guess Mom and Dad had lost interest as time passed.

I spoke up telling what I had heard in the car ride. "Huh, well, we were talking about staying all night while we were driving over."

Awkwardness engulfed the room, and the adults stared back at me in the same way you would look at a person who had just blurted out the darkest family secret. My mom made excuses and said she didn't know what I was talking about. We left, saying our goodbyes. I obliviously and happily leaped in the backseat of the car having enjoyed the evening. The drive, though, quickly became uncomfortable and quiet, like someone was sitting in the car completely naked and no one would name it. My mom broke the silence but not the uncomfortableness. She couldn't believe I would say such a thing to Dawn and Tim. I should be quiet. Children are to be seen and not heard, or some version of that line used for many millennia to keep kids from making awkward uncomfortable moments for adults.

"Well, that's what you said," I reasoned. Apparently, adults, at least my mother, can't be appealed to by reason.

My Dad pulled the car into Roland's driveway and turned off the engine. We all got out of the car, my sister and I pouring out of the backseat of the car. My Dad made his way to me and spanked my behind with his hand while I stood in the driveway. I was incredulous and surprised. What did I do?

"You need to learn to be quiet and leave the adults to do the talking," was the response.

For years to come, I realized that was another of those moments when I told the truth and got in trouble for it, the moments that sealed the way I felt about speaking up. I had simply said what was true, and the truth was met with violent response and anger. I had embarrassed my parents who said one thing and did another. To this day, I don't know why we left Dawn's house and didn't stay—what it was that made my parents exchange knowing glances that silently communicated, "Let's get out of here before she asks us to stay!" Or, maybe it was the realization that there was no room. Maybe it was something I can't even imagine. It may have been very legitimate.

Or not.

I cried myself to sleep that night. Dad's spankings, few though they were, never really hurt my butt as much as they embarrassed me or wounded my spirit in some way. The reality was that I did say what I had heard. Adults understand that not everything talked about in one setting is to be repeated in another. There are good reasons for that. However, to a nine-year-old, the only thing I knew was to say what was real. The adults in my life shamed that out of me. Don't trust that you know what is real—that internal message stuck. Don't trust that you heard correctly. Don't speak truth. Sit quietly. Let others do the talking. Let others decide what you will do. Let others deal with things. You, sit quietly.

"But, I heard that if there is an invitation to stay then we were …."

"Shhhh. Hush child. You don't know what you're talking about. Who would have said such a thing? No, that's not right. If it is, it's not to be spoken."

The next morning, the sun rose over the mountains as it had done every day. Birds chirped to greet the dawn of a new day's activity. The sun warmed the air while the breeze made the millions of leaves shimmer. Kids played. Adults talked and had coffee and got ready for work. Uncle Roland sat in his recliner watching it all.

Just like every other day.

I was not the same, though. The day before would be one I would not recover from for 47 years.

Hush child.

The lesson learned that night in Montana lodged inside me deeply. I was unsure if I could trust myself. I was unsure about what was expected of me from the adults in my life. It felt like I couldn't win a game that was stacked against me. I definitely couldn't navigate this uncertainty. It just got more difficult. Not only was I uncertain about what was expected of me from the adults in my life, but I was not sure what to expect of them. I began to feel that I was not enough.

Soon after we had returned home from Montana, we moved 80 miles south of where we had been living, school resumed, and life went on. My family lived in a house on the top of a hill accessible by a steep and long gravel drive. Below us were six other houses in the neighborhood developed and built by the same man who sold or rented each one. From the top of the hill, beautiful landscapes stretched out below, curving around hilltops in every direction.

This is where I rode my bike from the top of the gravel drive toward the road at the bottom past all the other houses. At least, that was my intention, before wiping out after just five yards due to a combination of the gravel and the speed of the bike. I was scraped up pretty bad. Mamaw was there when it happened. She was upset that her boy had gotten hurt. Dad was more like, "He seems ok, he can get up." Of course, Dad was right. I could get up and, even though banged up a bit, would live to try the feat on another day.

Spring had followed the fall and winter, and the sun was providing light later into the day. What a glorious time of year. Those longer days were bringing more warmth to the air. The windows were open in the living room, and a gentle breeze blew the curtains like waves lapping the shore of my favorite beach. I could smell through the screen door the grassy floral scents of a renewed earth after a long winter.

Ruth and I spent hours playing with Barbies and GI Joes. Our imaginations were endless when it came to pretend family structures and predicaments that could be contrived.

This evening found us playing in the living room. We had set up the dolls in a house with their camper, or van we now had determined, in the middle of the room. Mom was around the corner in the kitchen making dinner. Dad was in the garage tinkering with something as he would do nearly every night.

Dinner that night was fried chicken. The aroma of the greasy delightful staple in our family, mostly at Mamaw's house, made me feel warm. It was nearly perfect.

I went to the kitchen for a drink at just the wrong time. The grease from the hot cast iron skillet popped and spewed grease toward my mom. It was just a small amount, but it burned. Just then Mom used the two-pronged fork she was frying with and turned it into a weapon. Her anger focused on the chicken in the pan, she stabbed it and stabbed it with the fork with such force that the pan inched and moved across the stove. Mom was cussing that chicken and the grease.

My eleven-year-old self couldn't resist laughing. It was comical to see my mom killing the chicken with deathly stabs even though it was already dead and nearly ready to eat.

As I turned the corner to head back to the living room, I heard my mom say under her breath but loud enough, "Damn kid." Those words poked holes in me. They stabbed at my inner self.

It was then that my mom said loud enough for us to hear,

because that's always the way she said this phrase as often as she repeated it, "I wish I was on a desert island alone with just me and the dog."

Another stab to my soul. It was violent in a way. I laid down in the hallway between the kitchen and the living room. I stayed there on the tile floor no longer feeling nearly perfect. It furthered the divide between my mom and me. I thought about it for decades, well into my adult life. I was the "damn kid." A nuisance. I was disdained so completely that the one who brought me to life wanted to run away from me. Damn kid.

I have heard that voice say those words over and over. Not beloved kid. Not darling kid. Not awesome kid. Not smart kid. Not "my kid who knew every riddle." No, damned.

I've carried that soul shrinking moment with me into every board meeting. I've carried the reality of that evening with me into every other relationship. I've carried those words into places where others laughed. I am a nuisance who has nothing to contribute.

Even though I have accomplished much in my life and have made many difficult decisions and led groups of people in a variety of settings, in the back of my mind playing on repeat are those words. That feeling. The stabbing feeling that I am not wanted. The feeling of disdain from my own mother. She damned me that night to a lifetime of less-than. I have been trying to be worthy ever since. Maybe if I tried hard enough, she would say, "I'm so glad you are my awesome kid."

My life was not one of hugs from my parents. I have not one memory of hearing "I love you" from my parents until I was an adult.

As I lay on the floor, Mom finally came by me on her way

to the laundry room. "What are you doing laying here?" I got up silently, went to the living room, and started playing again.

My childhood was lived in a world of fantasy. The make-believe in my own mind was always on, nearly 24/7. I created my own reality where I was surrounded by people who loved me in my imaginary family. I created a reality where I was confident and could command starships, lead a fictional town, make my own way in the world, and be successful. I had to escape the damned and weave back together the disconnected threads of my self. I realized that, in my family, I was as silent and invisible as the breeze.

Nineteen

NOT ENOUGH

The silence in the car was deafening. The road passed beneath the tires with a rhythmic thumping. The fields on either side of the highway passed with speed as cows, oblivious to the travelers' presence, continued to graze. The sun was coming in the windshield at just the right place to be a nuisance. The downturned visor was no help. I tried to place it in various spots in front and to my right side, but at my height and the setting sun's spot on the horizon, nothing worked. So, I rode along with the evening sun in my eyes causing me to squint as if I were trying to read a distant billboard.

This was a typical trip on Route 23, which connects the northern part of the State of Ohio with Kentucky. This was the road my mom, dad, sister, and I traveled from Columbus to Beaver many weekends. Unfortunately, the silence was typical. Whenever it was just me and my dad in the car as it was on this occasion, it was like this. We were rarely alone, but when we were, I wondered what he thought would happen if he looked my direction. Would it be so bad if he just acknowledged my presence? Would our connection compete with the roar reminding us of the delicate balance holding the Rambler together and cause it simply to cease moving forward? Something that likely should have happened years before. Or, what if he said my name? Would a cow along the road stand up and take notice as if in celebration?

I will never know what would have happened. We rode along in silence. I assume the radio was on, but I can't remember. Our family listened to music in the car. If anyone was going to break with that tradition though, it would be my dad.

I felt as if I were invisible. That would be a great superpower to have, if it was only used for good. I wasn't going to save the world from destruction. Instead, I felt like I was going to slide into the seat. Most of the time, I just tried to ignore it or just acted as if nothing were wrong. I was just the Invisible Kid when dad was around. This was the way it was. This silence was pretty much a staple of Dad's method of handling most things. It was quite normal.

Riding along that day, I carried a feeling of discomfort around my dad that had transferred to others, a feeling that I would lug around. I expected silence when I was around other men. Silence is what I received from my dad, so why would I expect other men to be any different? I assumed the problem here was with me. I knew I was not like all of them. After all, I didn't care much for anything Dad, or other men, were interested in. Dad was a brick and block mason. I didn't identify. On the few occasions I went with him to work, I spent the day worrying and crying that my hands were dirty from the dry cement mix because, as it dried, it felt like they were shrinking. Dad liked football. I didn't quite get why that was exciting. Dad liked to fish. To me it was boring. Besides, once as a boy he caught the hook in my nose as he cast his line. I just didn't think we had much in common. Maybe Dad felt that too. He didn't know what to do with me. What do you talk about to a boy who doesn't like football, for God's sake?

He tried. He would throw a football for me to catch in the backyard, and I would duck. I was afraid it was so hard that it would hurt. And, if the ball did hit me, the pain and resulting bruise would be more than I wanted to bear. He was my Webelo den leader in Scouts. I was in scouts to be around other boys, hoping all those boy ways and boy games, like football, would rub off on me. Dad was even the Troop scout master for a time. My family, at the encouragement of the next door neighbors, really got into the scout scene, even going to the Jamboree.

I felt separate. Not boy enough. That didn't even change when I went to college or as an adult, or worked, or got married. I was the outsider around whom everyone else was silent out of uncertainty about how to talk to a boy like me. That was the story I told myself. That day in the southbound car was a prime example of the moments of silence that would define my life for decades to come. I didn't know until years later that Dad himself was never afforded a role model in his own father. He didn't know how to relate to me and was likely as uncomfortable as I was, which was why he opted for silence. It was, at least, familiar.

Grandpa Lykins loved all of his many kids on some level, I'm sure. Throughout my life, I saw him upset with himself when he thought he'd hurt their feelings, yet clearly not sure what to do about that. The family gathered around to hear the stories of the past that he would spin every family gathering at his house. Those stories are still repeated at Lykins family gatherings by Grandpa's sons and daughters. I've heard them so many times they have become familiar signposts along the road of my life. Once in a while, new ones are discovered, which does keep the journey interesting.

The way I understand it, Dad was the only son who would work for Grandpa. Since Dad was willing, Grandpa took him up on it. Grandpa put high expectations on Dad to perform. Even in bad weather, Grandpa would have Dad outside doing jobs for him. On one occasion, Dad wasn't doing a task correctly, and in response, Grandpa swung a long board and hit Dad on his head, near his left ear. To this day, Dad at 80 years old still has trouble with his hearing and dizziness as a result.

Dad didn't have a great relationship with Grandpa, who didn't talk to him except when he needed something. Grandpa was a force in the world. He was a force in the Lykins family. That force was not always a good one. Grandpa was good at telling others in the family, especially daughters-in-law, what they should or shouldn't do, or think, or wear, or what color the women should have on their nails. He was a man of strong opinions and was always willing to share them.

Maybe silence is the best deal given the other options modeled for Dad by his own father. For me, it felt like a board to the head anyway. Being shut out from this man who was the only person I had to help me maneuver the life of a boy and being a male in the world sucked the sound right out of my life.

That did change as I got older, was married, and my first child, Beth, was born. During the first months of Beth's life, Dad worked on a masonry job in Columbus, where Shelly and I lived. Dad would stay with us a few nights each week instead of taking the south bound route an hour and a half home. He and Mom had moved back to Beaver, across the road from Mamaw and Papaw's house. After Mamaw's death, they moved into a small trailer on Papaw's farm, which was the last dwelling they would ever share together.

On those weekly overnight visits, Dad would eat dinner with us and spend time playing with Beth. Over time, he started talking to me. I began to feel comfortable asking him about his day and the job he was doing. We talked. Over many years, I ended up with a great relationship with my dad. He is a rock in my life. He consistently says he loves me and is proud of me, words I longed to hear so many years ago riding along Route 23. He calls to talk. He comes to visit me during afternoons sometimes, even when we have lived nearly two hours away. He still visits. We spend the day together eating, shopping, talking. He is the best Papaw to my daughters. He is a great father-in-law to Shelly. He is a great dad to me.

I know now that I have always been important to him, and he wishes things had been different in those early years. I am just grateful for new roads to travel with a companion who acknowledges my presence, asks me how I am doing, and gives great hugs. The cows would stand up and celebrate for our great new relationship.

Even though my relationship with Dad was improving, his relationship with Mom was unraveling. I admit, I wasn't sure how this change for them would affect me. That made me apprehensive. It was indicative of the instability that had been part of our family for as long as I remembered. I think that Dad was likely the same way with Mom that he was with me. There was a lot of silence in many ways. He kept to himself, coming home and doing his own thing. When they needed to interact to get a question answered, make a plan, or eat a meal, they interacted. I don't recall any big fights or arguments. I think my parents kind of existed and managed a family but didn't really open up to each other. Like many other couples, financial stress caused a burden that was hard to overcome. It added to the instability. I wonder if they (Mom in particular) were looking for a life or relationship where each person mattered—where a couple shared life in an intimate way. I think there was an exhaustion that came from just getting by, and that eventually led them to split once and for all. Mom wanted out, and Dad, not one to put up a fight for anything, gave up and let her have what she wanted. Maybe he knew there was no point in trying to win something where Mom is concerned.

My mom summoned us home for the weekend to tell us about the divorce plan. Shelly and I, along with our one-year-old daughter, Beth, lived in Wilmore, Kentucky, where I was attending seminary. I knew something was up, and there was going to be a talk during the weekend. The topic wasn't all that obvious though. I had no idea the plan was to tell my sister and me that our family structure and history was being altered permanently.

They had separated for a short few months while I was in seventh grade. We split up the household goods, furniture, and kids. Ruth went with Mom. I went with Dad. We lived about a half hour apart. Mom had an apartment on the top floor of a house that had been divided. Dad and I lived in a trailer, barely talking to each other. He worked. I cooked and did the dishes and cleaned. Each night long and lonely, but not hopeless. At first it was kind of fun. An adventure.

Mom and Dad had been married when she was 17 and just out of high school. Most teen marriages don't work out, but usually they end before two and a half decades pass. They didn't really fight. It was more that my mom would be unhappy and upset over something and Dad would leave her alone. Dad spent most nights in the garage, even if Mom was fuming in the house. Avoidance was his default coping method.

One night Dad and I were at Mom and Ruth's apartment for dinner and the evening. Dad decided to stay all night. I had not brought clothes to make that work. No pajamas, no toothbrush, nothing. With no place to sleep except on the couch, I lay down in my clothes and my anger. I was mad. Why didn't they make up their mind instead of pulling us back and forth? When we arrived, a man was at my mom's place talking with her about cleaning her carpets. My Dad, nearly immediately, had him by the collar, fist drawn. It ended with no one hit or hurt. The one time he fought was for her.

Mamaw and Papaw were not happy with Mom. They rarely ever were happy with her. They blamed it all on Mom. They usually did blame most anything that went wrong on Mom.

"How could Ann let a man like Lee Lykins get away," they said. They often tried to get me to tell them details of what was going on.

By year's end we were all back together, everything from both living places placed on one truck and moving to Columbus, again.

Other than that, a divorce was really not something I expected. I mean, everything felt okay. I visited with my family one weekend each month. We had holidays together, and it all seemed fine. Apparently not really. I still don't know all that precipitated the split.

Dad met Louise a short time later. Dad connected with Louise really fast, and I could see why. She fit into our family well. It was all a bit awkward, though, with the quick timing.

I had hardly gotten used to the idea of my parents being divorced when I also had to get used to a new person stepping into our lives. The time from divorce to Dad and Louise's wedding day was like watching a time-lapse video of a seed growing into a mature plant. The wedding was only a few months after the divorce was finalized. The ceremony was very nice, though it felt a bit odd to watch my dad pledge his faithfulness to someone who wasn't Mom. Still, I was glad when they asked me to say a prayer during the wedding. That afternoon, I prayed about new beginnings. We had cake and punch and celebrated. My dad and new stepmom were both well known in the community of Jackson, where Louise had lived for many years and where Dad was moving to join her in her house. The church that Dad and Mom had attended became Dad and Louise's church, even though Dad was asked to vacate his board seat when it was discovered he was going through a divorce. After all, how could a man be a leader if he couldn't take care of and manage his own life, or rather, wife, in this case. I'm sure that was on everybody's mind. It did say something like that in the Bible.

Dad and his new bride left for their honeymoon, and I was tasked with checking on and locking up the trailer on Mamaw and Papaw's farm in Beaver where my parents had lived and where Dad had been living since their split. The place was small but cozy, and my mom had decorated it to be very welcoming and homey in the country theme that was popular at the time. I stopped on my way back to seminary in Kentucky and said goodbye to the house mom and dad shared for three years. Never my home, exactly. I never lived there. I spent weekends there and many holidays. But, once the reception was over, the punch and cake cleaned up, and Dad and Louise gone to some destination to begin a new life together, I was left holding the key. Ruth and I had just thrown Mom and Dad a 25th anniversary party a year earlier. It was a smashing success. I still joke that if they had only let us know they were that close to a divorce it would have saved us a lot of trouble and money. But, this day was no joke.

As I prepared to leave the house and lock it up, I wondered where the family Christmas decorations were. Some of them I had made. The glass blue ball ornament with 1972 glued with gold glitter on the side I made in cub scouts; it was an heirloom. Mom just left most things and walked away. Dad was beginning a new life, and he and Louise had gone through the trailer and tossed things they would not need. Both very legitimate responses. But I was feeling less than legitimate that evening. It was like being left behind. Twenty-five years of family life in boxes for others to go through. I turned the key and realized this was the end of an era. It was the end of 25 years of family tradition, even the tradition of Dad hiding out in the garage was over. It had all changed. I locked the door, shut it behind me, and cried.

Over the years, Louise became an important part of our family. She really was committed to all of us as if we had always been in her life. I appreciate that and her for the way she has loved my dad and the rest of us equally well. Mom soon had a new man in her life too. That was a lot of whiplash to endure in a few months' time. My mom's man friend was around for several years. They never married. He cheated on her with another family member who was younger than me. He was followed by another man who she did marry. He was in our lives for more than a decade. He became Papaw Stan to my kids. I always enjoyed him. I actually performed the entire wedding service for him and Mom. I would joke with people, "I married my mother." If they only knew that, in our family's past, that isn't so farfetched for some family members. Stan and Mom divorced in 2013 after he had treated her badly for years. Apparently, he wasn't as nice behind my back as he was to my face. Mom married Byron after that. It is too early to tell, but so far so good. I think he'll stay around. Mom finally seems to be content.

We moved often while I was growing up. Many houses, towns, and schools have been in my life. My parents were never quite happy, even if Dad was whistling most times as he headed out to the garage, there was an underlying sense of being unsettled, something not said, something never dealt with. I realized I really could only count on one thing. Mamaw and Papaw would be in the same house on the same road, with open arms, money in its hiding place, and food to eat. That was the one constant. Of course, I know now how chaotic and unhealthy they were too. Maybe that's what I could count on. Chaos!

I guess I could count on me. That's it. Just like that fall day on Beaver Pike in southeast Ohio, I locked up, cleaned up, took care. Responsible me. I haven't yet figured out all the pieces to that puzzle. I still am overburdened by a sense of responsibility for everyone else. I know that is an impossible task I've aspired to achieve, much like two young people, one only 17 years old, getting married and moving the chaos from their childhood homes with them into their marriage in 1962.

Twenty

CONDEMNED OR WAS IT SAVED?

D espite the large empty area of grass and parking, many people drove past and didn't even notice the church that sat a few yards off the road. The building was not that noticeable. It was beige, not very big, bricked front, the rest just painted block. It was a two story building with a steeple that my dad had built in our basement and placed on the roof himself, likely with some help from a couple of guys from the congregation. This church was where I spent much of my youth. We went every time the doors opened, and in that church they opened a lot.

The small sanctuary was on the second floor, seating nearly 200 people if everyone packed in shoulder to shoulder, which was rare on any occasion. The fellowship hall and classrooms were on the lower level. I had spent the last seven years, from 1975-1982, in this small congregation. During that time there had been five pastors ranging widely in personalities and styles of leading and preaching.

I only remember one woman from the congregation who ever preached, Sister Elsie Lutz, though I never dared call her Elsie. Even though women were never pastors, Sister Lutz preached once in a while. I thought it was so strange, her standing in a place only men occupied. She was a short woman with a powerful force. She wore dresses all the time. They looked much like my Mamaw's dresses that she made for herself. Sister Lutz also had very short hair. So, she obviously believed a woman should not wear pants but didn't belong to the women-should-not-cut-their-hair sect. Both, among other varieties of outward appearance code, were found among the women of our church.

Sister Lutz, like most other preachers who stepped into our church's pulpit, talked about sin mostly. It was defined by rules of dress, music preference, alcohol consumption, dancing, movie attending, and much more, but I don't think I need to go on with the list of vices that would land you straight in hell with other players of games with dice. Not much of anything was left off the list. I'm not sure what was allowed, but I didn't really give much thought to it. That is the way it was. Jesus was the cosmic eye in the sky who cared about every action or inaction of your life. Oh, not cared as in compassionately interested, but cared in order to keep track in a grand universal book that would one day be opened to see if you would be damned or not. Most of us worried that we would not make it through that scrutiny. Or, we didn't think about it and did whatever and would get saved every once in a while when the preacher would guilt people to come forward and kneel to pray. Altar calls were a regular part of our worship. In most worship services there would be a moment at the end of the service when the preacher would ask people to come down front, kneel at a railing, and pray. The preacher would have us stand, sing a song, and wait for people to come forward to kneel in the front of the church and pray to get saved. They would confess to God that they believed in Jesus and ask Jesus to forgive all the sin they had committed. Then, they would be expected to be different. Not as much jewelry and makeup, change their music, dancing, movie going, those kinds of things. Nearly every worship service ended that way.

The issue became how difficult it was to live up to the expectations of the church after that moment. The expectation was that we would need to eventually get saved again. The journey from altar to heaven was both boring and full of stress. Getting saved over and over was just good practice in case you missed confessing the occasional forgotten sin.

There were other church members who, like Sister Lutz, influenced me in many ways. We did have fun--our own kind of fun. We laughed, hung out, talked while kneeling in the hard wooden pews during prayer time, and we lived life together. We went to worship three times a week and threw in a revival for an entire week once in a while for good measure. That way, God would know we were serious about our faith. After all, look at how much we were willing to sacrifice for God and church. Maybe that would get noticed by Jesus and marked down in the big book and outweigh the moments when someone might walk through the wine aisle at the grocery store.

Even though my understanding of God and even Jesus now is quite different than it was in the 1970s at this church, these folks were the people who nurtured my foundation. These preachers, even if I heard a lot more about judgement and fire than love and grace, were the ones who shaped me. After the second sermon of the day, Sunday nights would find me looking out the open windows of the sanctuary watching the hundreds of fireflies in the field right outside.

I knew God had it in for non-Christians, sinners,

heathens, all of them wicked. I heard Sister Lutz say to her Sunday School class one week, "I don't pray for forgiveness of sin because I don't sin." Even as a very young adult, I was impressed and yet skeptical. Although, if she wasn't aware, there were people who would have disagreed with her since she cut her hair short after all, and some thought that was a sin for sure. A woman's hair was her crowning glory (or something like that). Even though she only wore dresses, a mark of holiness, she wore short sleeves, a suspect crossing of the lines for some.

It really didn't take much to be labelled a sinner in this church. Compared to many of the church members, I would have been considered a person who practiced at this sin thing. I was a more "worldly" part of the flock. It was a designation I didn't mind at all. The Bible says to sin boldly, and I did. I blasted my rock music records. I went to movies. I watched television shows like "Dallas." I played Monopoly. I even cursed once in a while. It was my rebellious time—not the drugs, women, and rock-and-roll kind of sinning or rebellion—more of an, I went to movies and admitted it kind of rebellion. It took me a while to give in to the "getting saved" expectation. In other places in my life, I was picked on and the outcast. Here in this church group, I was accepted as one of the group and yet could be a bit bad ass (since it didn't take much). There was so much shame heaped on us. I kind of wore my status as a sinner and unsaved proudly. It set me apart in ways that felt powerful. It was one way I felt I had some power to say, "This is me, deal with it."

Of course, I was not a bad kid. I was not a bad young adult. Actually, is anyone a bad anything at any age? I guess there are bad behaviors. There are horrendous actions. Maybe people who murder are bad people, or maybe they just haven't been introduced to their goodness. No one has yet revealed to them that they are a good person. Maybe someone in their life has told them they are bad, evil, shameful. Then they act out of that self-concept. I'm not sure, but that's my current Methodist belief-system coming out, a belief-system I wouldn't embrace until graduate school.

Even my grandparents, who did terrible things to me physically and emotionally, were not bad people. They were wounded people. They were disturbed. They shouldn't have been around children, for sure. I have no idea what happened to them in their past. I know nothing about what influenced them, how their parents were toward them or what insecurities they encountered. Knowing my family's propensity for shutting up and avoiding truth and conversation, it is no surprise I don't know. Now I will never know.

I did not do any really bad things when I was a teen or young adult. I have always been a guy who does what is expected and follows the rules. But I had this idea that I was not good. I only heard about the depravity of humanity, which included me. Shame was pervasive, and it seeped into me. I held on to it and believed the lie that I was bad in my core.

God was another story. I was scared of God. To me, God was not much different than the abusers who posed as loving adults in my life. Or, those who abandoned me to figure life out on my own who were waiting to say, "I told you you weren't enough," at the first sign of faltering. I was taught that sin was about actions that did not conform to the rules of the church and the expectations of God. If my actions did not conform to the rules of the church, then God was as displeased as anyone else. I knew God wanted me to conform. That was the norm. I needed to get on board like everyone else did, because then I'd be a happy and fulfilled person in life and even after I died.

One weekend, another congregation in our denomination had a camp meeting complete with a big tent, quartet music, and a well-known preacher who would draw people out on a Friday night. It is interesting to look back and realize that the only folks interested in this kind of event were those who already were saved and all-in, along with the teens and children who had no choice but to be in this tent on a summer night. This particular Friday night landed during the week of my cousin Sandy's annual visit to my house in Columbus. Every summer for a few days in a row, we would spend the week shopping for her school clothes, seeing movies, swimming, laughing, and eating chips and catsup. However, this night, we were taken to the camp meeting.

We sat in rows of folding chairs under the lights of the tent. Fans flapped back and forth in the hands of most attendees as they tried to ward off the summer heat, even though it was a nice touch reminding us of hell. The preacher was riled up over a full page of letters published earlier that week in *The Columbus Dispatch* newspaper written by homosexuals (that is the term used by us and the paper) with the nerve to ask for basic and equal civil rights for the LGBTQ+ community. The preacher was having none of it. He saw right through their propaganda to their real agenda of poisoning the minds of our youth and destroying the very fabric of our society. If God had meant for there to be homosexuals with rights, God would have created Adam and Steve instead of Adam and Eve. But God didn't do that, so we should write *The Dispatch* our own letters and put forth a united Christian front showing these gay folks and everyone else how righteous we were and how very, very, very sinful and evil and hell-bound they were.

The preacher ended with the expected altar call. I stood

there in front of my folding chair with everyone else, my heart pounding. In my introvertedness, I didn't want to go forward in front of everyone, but I made a deal with God. If God would allow me to get home and make it to bedtime before a car hit me and I died, I'd pray before I went to sleep. I was staying in my sister's room while Sandy visited. We kids stayed up late on that Friday night, but I kept my part of the deal. God had indeed been kind enough not to come back and rapture the good people during that time, leaving me and Sue Babbet behind. Everyone knew Sue Babbet would not be going to heaven since she wore an ankle bracelet.

After everyone else went to bed, I knelt and prayed for God to forgive my sins in the name of Jesus. I remember I was expecting some emotional outburst, like I'd witnessed in worship on occasions. It didn't happen like that. I got up from kneeling and walked to the window. Looking out at the dark night sky and the bright moon, I started to laugh. It was a deep laugh of release. I just felt happy. Joyful may be a better term for it; it was deeper than happiness. I knew I was forgiven, and God was right there. It was not the first night I prayed. Even though you can't quite put your finger on it as a little boy or a teen, you know when you aren't quite the same as everyone else was, or was pretending to be anyway. You know when you think you masturbate more than anyone else and God surely would make your life miserable now as well as write it down in the Book due to the frequency. You know you're different when you find other boys attractive. You can't stop staring at them. Their jaw line, those eyelashes, the wide wrist, hairy muscular legs, bubble butts.

I could not say anything about that. I could not let anyone, even God, in on the hidden truth stuffed down so far inside me. I had heard the preachers. I had heard the Sunday

School teachers who didn't even sin at all, let alone have these feelings. So, I prayed for years to be released from these wrong feelings, relegating my own self to the abominable category.

The next day I wrote my letter to *The Dispatch* and said I was disappointed they would give newspaper space to homosexuals. I wrote a letter about God hating a sinful lifestyle and giving the "other side" equal room in the paper. God was appalled, and homosexuals were abhorrent. It clearly said so in the Bible, if *The Dispatch* would have just checked. I wanted to be part of this righteous display of witness to the evils of a sinful world. After all, these gay people were going to shove a godless lifestyle down our throats, and the moral fibers holding together our country and society would be shredded. So, yes. Count me in, I thought. For this chance to be part of the group in this way, I wanted to do it. I so wanted and desired acceptance that I would even write a letter condemning a part of myself. I kept that newspaper page in my scrapbook for many years.

Thinking back now, I can clearly see the conflict that was going on inside me. It was a conflict I wouldn't fully embrace for decades. I so desired to be accepted by this church community and God that I allowed my own reality to be pushed down and denied and wrote a letter condemning who I was. In spite of that conflict, I really did align my life with God that Friday night when I prayed to be saved, and I have been unpacking or deconstructing that decision ever since. Looking back on it now, our concept of sin was a list of inconsequential actions to avoid that did not amount to a hill of beans. Who really cared that I went to watch "Star Wars" or other movies? Obviously, many people were judging me for that simple thing. Still, I went to the movies. Even after I prayed to be saved, I still went to movies. No one had to say anything, although sometimes they would, for me to know that was against the rules and I was a sinner. I heard preachers mention it in sermons. But no one really had to say so. I knew. I knew I was living what was a lie. I was not a good Christian, because I had a double life--good saved boy and movie goer. That was the battle inside me.

That is as bad as my sins ever were, yet I was surrounded by a culture that helped me feel condemned. I didn't even smoke, which was considered a higher level of sinful action than going to movies. Even though I didn't know how to express it, the fact that I knew I liked guys ate at me. It was a secret that I didn't know what to do with, and it was on the big serious part of the rules list. On the inside I battled against the voices that were louder than my own. I suppressed the voice of my reality for the people in my life. I denied what I was for the Church. Ultimately, I gave up myself for God. I thought that was what he wanted. After all, God didn't even want me to enjoy a movie in the cinema, television, rock music, or games with dice. I did all of that and hid even bigger truth that dare not be spoken.

God was wrathful and angry, and I had to show God that I was not bad. But how? I really didn't know. Read my Bible daily. Pray daily. Go to church when it was offered. Go to special revival services. It was not enough to take away the pull that separated me from myself.

Sin I never committed wrecked my life. Now I know that the sin was not mine. It was the church's. I was a good boy. I am a good man. God loved me unconditionally. That truth is all that matters. I wish I had learned that earlier.

PART FIVE

BELONGING

Twenty-One

INTERNAL BATTLE

Early in my marriage to Shelly, there were several times that I left the house to blow off steam. I got in my car and drove. I made my way to the nearest freeway entrance ramp and went as fast as I felt I could. I rolled the windows down if it was warm enough, and I cranked up the radio and escaped.

I don't know what I was escaping. I was running away from something that kept me in turmoil and uncertainty. I would just have these moments when I needed to scream at the universe. That was better than screaming at my family, although I did that sometimes too.

I'm sure Shelly didn't know what to do and what to make of her husband. Beth and Elyse, my daughters, had no idea what was going on when they were little girls. There was one time that Beth, a teenager, wanted a certain prom dress that cost much more money than I was willing to spend. She said, "I never get anything I want." Even though that's a classic line teens say to their parents, including me to mine, I lost it. I reminded her very intensely that I had just bought a car so she could have the sporty, black Pontiac Grand Am I was driving.

Our family survived and even thrived, but I could be intense. I wished I could have helped those in my life understand what was going on when I would get in those moods, but I couldn't. I didn't quite know myself. I was a man who never fit in, who was made to feel he was responsible for other people's well-being, who carried around memories of abuse and rejection. Those were burdens that became too much. They weighed me down. The pressure came out sometimes like the release valve on a pressure cooker.

It came out in other ways too. There were church meetings, several actually, where I would dismiss myself to just walk off and tighten the valve down before it blew.

I was told once in a salary discussion, "All you need to buy is your food."

I was told once that I was wasting money because they had noticed the outdoor lights on either side of the garage on the parsonage (the church-owned house where the pastor lived) had been left on through the day. I responded by asking if I could have Christmas tree lights, since they didn't serve any purpose either. There are many more moments like those where I just left the room to deal with my feelings.

Throughout my life, I wanted to fit in. I just wanted to be accepted and included by those who were telling me that I was "other." Different. Not like everyone else.

Shape up. Get on board. Straighten up.

The inadequacies I felt and concealed created such conflict in me. I was exhausted from portraying strength on the outside, coupled with the fight on the inside. Eventually, I didn't want to keep it up any longer. I had to be authentic and real if I was to be able to stand comfortably in my own skin and let my voice inhabit my body and being.

Twenty-Two

THE BEST WE COULD

The summer I prayed to be saved was in 1977. I attended public school up to that point, but that was the year I started high school at Central Christian Academy (CCA), another place, another group of people, who influenced my life deeply. I am still friends with many of those former CCA students. Several I would say are some of my best friends, even though I don't see them very often at all now. Most have loved me and shown me grace that I did not personally know at that small church in those earlier years.

CCA was a new Christian school in its second year of existence started by and housed in a church that was not too far from our home. We knew some of the staff and students. It was purported to be an environment where Christian kids could be safe from the corrupting influence of the world. The Bible and religion were part of the curriculum and structure. We were required to attend chapel each week. To apply for special privileges, like extra break time, students could memorize a monthly scripture. The total student body was around 100 students, starting in kindergarten through senior high. It fluctuated each year depending on which students returned and which did not, whether they had chosen to go back to public school or maybe couldn't afford the tuition.

I really liked going to school at Central Christian Academy. I met some awesome friends. I was not teased. It was a place where I excelled and became a leader. I started a student council. Through the student council we planned parties, like 50's Day, Valentine's, and any other reason we could come up with to get out of classwork for a few hours. We held fundraisers and started sports teams. The volleyball team, which I played on, was our first foray into sports. We advanced to basketball and softball. We started a yearbook and a newsletter.

We even held Junior-Senior Banquets (a version of a prom, but we couldn't call it a prom because it was not to be associated with what other non-Christian schools did). The school was small enough that we ended up calling them High School Banquets and letting every high school student attend. I never dated girls during high school except for attending the Banquets at the end of each year. My graduating class in 1981 consisted of me and one girl. The ceremony was held in the sanctuary of the church, which is where we held all of our all-school gatherings. We laughed that we didn't want it to seem like we were getting married walking down the middle aisle. When the ceremony was over, I left that evening knowing the school would always have a place in my heart. I even went so far as to declare a major in elementary education so I could return to teach at Central Christian Academy and continue the legacy.

Things didn't work out that way. I changed my major a couple of times in college. During one phase, I was going to be an accountant and was working at an accounting firm while taking classes. I loved the people and the work I was doing there. However, it was then that I started having a sense of being unsettled. I was at my desk one afternoon, and I had a heavy feeling. I actually got weepy. I knew I couldn't do the work of an accountant the rest of my life. I wanted to do something that directly involved helping people. That's the best I could describe it. I wasn't accustomed to paying attention to my feelings. I had pushed them down and denied them for so many years.

I changed my major to social work and graduated college with a degree in Social Work. I applied for many jobs but did not have any luck. During one interview the interviewer asked, "Where do you see yourself in five years?" I answered, "Using my gifts and skills in the church somehow." When I returned to my car I thought, "Where did that come from?" I knew once I let it sink in that it went all the way back to my time in high school. At that time, being rooted even more than I had been before in the beliefs of our church increased my passion for its work and led to my first feelings of being called to preach. Even though I would later understand the negative view of God and even myself that this church had over me, it was all I knew. This was how God was, I assumed. This is how church was, I assumed. One Father's Day, I made a plaque for my dad that had my picture and a scripture verse, "Go into all the world and preach the gospel" (Mark 16:15). I have wondered if at the time I wanted my dad's approval and acceptance and for him to be proud of me. I wonder if that's how I thought about God too. If I were a preacher, a pastor specifically, maybe Dad and God would finally accept me.

I didn't lead worship or have any opportunities to preach during my high school years, though I was an integral part of leading the youth ministry at our home church. This feeling came out of a desire to do something bigger than I was already doing for God. I didn't think of it this way then, but I also wonder if I wanted to create safe spaces for other people like I had experienced. Throughout my teen years, Christian spaces were safe for me. I felt a sense of belonging I had not known otherwise. There was genuine community, even if it was tempered with an underlying culture of judgement. I only realized recently the underlying culture betrayed by a line of our school song, "We study hard to show ourselves approved." There it is yet again—the accepted pressure to live up to an ideal, or to try harder to be accepted by God and others.

CCA still has an important place in my heart. I grew a lot during my four years there, and it was a great place to go to school. I wouldn't quite fit today if the school were still open (it closed two years after I graduated). I have changed so much. My beliefs have changed. And, I have experienced church as not such a safe space. Once I actually became a pastor eight years later, I started to understand that not all Christian spaces or churches were safe spaces. I have been part of some great moments. I get to be part of people's lives in the most vulnerable and intimate times—births, illness, divorce, death. I have celebrated milestones, prayed over trees planted in a town park, prayed for city council meetings. I have met some awesome people.

And, I have encountered some angry and manipulative people. What a letdown. Many people who are part of churches do not follow Jesus, even though they claim to. There, that's my judgement. As a pastor, I have been pushed around, disrespected, dismissed, yelled at, and cussed at. We had our problems at Central Christian Academy, but we were trying to be the best we could, and we cared about each other.

"We believe in God above and Jesus' love and in His Spirit too," our school song began.

On some deep level, I still do.

Twenty-Three

~~~

CLUELESS

I started my college years in a small town at a small school in central Kentucky, just west of Lexington in Wilmore. Most of the buildings and businesses seemed like they hadn't changed since the ribbon cutting for the new stop along the Cincinnati Southern railroad line in 1876. In 1890, Asbury College was founded, and it also didn't seem to have changed much. Of course, I exaggerate, but there is no denying that life in Wilmore, Kentucky, was a walk back to earlier and easier days. The biggest happening that pushed on that idyllic, protected world was the arrival of a couple thousand students for the college and seminary every fall—a shock to an aging and genteel system, although the money the students brought to town was a welcome thing, for sure. We were ready to spend at the IGA or at the Sims Drug store, which still had a soda fountain and lunch counter.

I liked it there. I hung out through the week with a group of about five other students of a variety of ages, class rankings, and grade levels. Although no one really talked about it much, I am pretty sure we had a variety of socio-economic statuses as well. There were the students who clearly came from more modest monetary resources, like myself. There were others who wore clothes that were tailored, sleek, and designer. Most of those friends lived close enough they went home each weekend.

Gavin was one of that group who lived down the road in Lexington, Kentucky. I enjoyed hanging out with Gavin. I was able to go home with him a couple of times when he needed to run into Lexington to get something he forgot or just to have dinner. Although to college students there is no "just to" casual shrugging off of free food. There are just times when you need something besides cafeteria food. It was still nice to get off campus. It was good to see another world than one I was used to experiencing. Upper middle class homes, cars, clothes. I was pretty sure Gavin didn't have to call home occasionally to tell his mom that the quarter tuition, room, and board bill had to be paid by a certain day to have her answer, "Well, I don't know what I'm supposed to do about it." I never understood that answer since I was here at this quaint private school four hours from home because my mom suggested it or, actually, insisted on it. It wasn't that I minded or put up much resistance to the idea. I was glad to get away from home and start out on a new journey in a setting similar to my high school years at a private Christian school. I could remain sheltered from the reality of dealing with people who were not like me or who did not hold the same beliefs. That was a big relief.

Gavin and I talked a lot. We spent time discussing our home church experiences. During one conversation he said, "The people in my church think that being a Christian means going to Zondervan once in a while." Zondervan being a national chain Christian bookstore at the time. Gavin came from a large United Methodist Church in Lexington. That was another world I didn't understand or even know existed. Apparently, there were churches that were not so hung up on the rules of no dancing, drinking, rock music, country music, or anything fun. This must have been what my elders from my home church had warned me of when they said Asbury was a, gasp, "liberal" school. Oh my God (oops), it was anything but. I admit, by the standards I brought with me, it was not so conservative, but to many other people not entrenched in the evangelical Christian church, it was downright draconian. That was its main charm to my mom. Asbury had a reputation of conservatively engaging students for Jesus. A feat attempted from the first day on campus. It was all Jesus all the time, at least on the outside.

I finished the academic year at Asbury College. Even though I enjoyed being there for many reasons, it was also very difficult. I ended up in a counselor's office for the first time in my life. Winter quarter was rough. I struggled with depression. I spent time alone most weekends. You would always find me at the social events and concerts that took place on campus, but I was there by myself. I started having health issues. A local doctor in Wilmore diagnosed me with a heart palpitation, which meant tests over Christmas break, including testing for low-blood sugar, or hypoglycemia. That was the beginning of what was diagnosed as type-1 diabetes 30 years later.

When I went home for summer, I ended up staying. I really just preferred the surroundings of my familiar world. At 20 years old in college, now at The Ohio State University while living at home, I was back in the congregation of my teen years. In the same church, with Sister Lutz and the rest of the gang, I became the volunteer youth leader. It was through that church that I met Shelly Richardson. We went to a Columbus Clippers baseball game together. She had been invited by her family members, who were acquaintances of mine. After that, we hung around each other for a year as friends. Included in our circle of three was a woman I had known for five years before. All of us became good, platonic, single friends. We talked, went to movies, enjoyed going out to eat, and hung around church together before and after worship. We did whatever good conservative Christian young people do or don't do.

After a few months of that, I began to miss Shelly when we weren't together. I thought of her when I woke up each morning. I anticipated spending time with her. I started to interpret those feelings as love and began to think that we should get married. I asked Shelly in May of that same year if we could change our relationship to be more than friends and she said yes.

Just a few weeks later, on a Thursday night when Shelly had her bowling league, I asked if I could pick her up from her apartment and take her to the bowling alley. I found a place to park my car and made my way up the steep flight of stairs to the second floor where Shelly's apartment was located. When she opened the door, she saw that I had on a suit, which was a bit overdressed for bowling. She knew something was up. We drove to a city park, which was used frequently by the school I had attended and graduated from just a couple of years before. I chose the location because I was familiar with it and knew there was a pond in the center of the park. On the banks of that pond, I got down on one knee and gave her the ring. At first, I pulled out my class ring to be funny harkening back to high school days of "going steady." But I did produce a modest diamond that I was proud of. She said yes, and I dropped her off at her bowling game. I don't know why I didn't stay. It never occurred to me to stay and watch her bowl, maybe be with her, back then. I went about my business, going home to tell my family how it went. At the time her league was finished, I picked her up, met her friends, and drove her back to her apartment. I went home to my parent's house. Three months later was our wedding day.

Those months between were full of stress. We planned everything ourselves. I don't remember how we came to that decision, although for me there would have been no other choice. I wouldn't leave the details of such an event open for someone else to get wrong. We went to tastings, appointments, and on shopping excursions. We made calls and tracked down the folks we wanted to provide those essential services that made up a wedding in the 1980s. We addressed each invitation. We bought the pastel butter mints and mixed nuts. We bought the ingredients for the red fruit punch.

When it came time to think about a best man to stand up with me at my wedding, Gavin was who I settled on. I really didn't have many male friends. Not really close friends anyway. Not the "I love you man, you've always been there for me. Will you do me the honor?" kind of friend. Gavin was as close as they came for me at the time, even though I hadn't seen him or talked to him since I left Kentucky. Gavin agreed to be my best man, and our mutual friend Marcus rode from Lexington to Columbus with him to attend the wedding. I hadn't seen these guys even once for about a year.

I woke on the morning of our wedding with a mixture of feelings. Outside, it was any normal September Saturday, even though it was a holiday weekend. The sky was a bit gray with the promise of clouds, sun, and no rain. I was pleased. I would have chosen such a day months ago when we started planning. I like to plan (some would say control) everything, but my control impulse is more about fear of being judged than it is control. It's more that I feel responsible for everything going the way it is planned. That is a huge responsibility on one person's shoulders, but I carried it with me. If I can control as much as possible, or plan it, or hold it close, I can minimize the opportunities people have of judging me for it. I have been convinced over my entire life that I will upset someone, or they will not like me and, therefore, reject me. My fear played out on that day and for many days, as it would for years to come, giving the happily ever after of our wedding and marriage a run for its money.

Shelly and I were married in the small church we attended with the steeple my dad had built. I had been a part of that congregation with my family since I was in seventh grade. My mom hosted the rehearsal dinner at our house the night before. I don't even remember what she served for dinner. I do remember the stress she was under because of the whole thing. Throughout the week of the wedding, she would direct her own stress and frustration toward me. The night before the rehearsal day, she said some biting angry comment to me about not wanting to do this and how she felt overwhelmed by all she had to do. I had gone to bed crying, and she came to my room, sat on the end of the bed, and apologized, yet again.

"You must not be very sorry, or you would actually change your behavior and stop," I said to her.

She couldn't argue with that, not that she was trying. This was not the first time her own emotions ended up causing her to take jabs at me, being the closest person in her presence at the time. I couldn't figure out how, but I thought maybe it was me who had put her in this position. I felt responsible that everything work out and that everyone be okay. I was both angry at her and burdened by the thought that it was my fault. Even though I really couldn't put it into words back then, I never understood what it was that brought them to the decision to let me live with Mamaw and Papaw and be gone for so much of my childhood. Why my mom and I clashed over the years over so many things was a mystery to me. However, looking back, I know, the anger that was deep in me had been pushed down and become a part of our interactions. That moment on the edge of my bed the week of my wedding, my mom was acting out of her own brokenness. She had no idea how to deal with or heal all the emotion and fear and anger that was in her. It came spilling out onto other people in her life, blaming them for her discontent. She lived with so many unresolved issues that ate at her and took bites out of the rest of us. I carried around my own brokenness from years of rejection and judgement from her and many others. I wonder if she and I had a troubled history because I represented her past in some way. I reminded her that she was not the mother she had hoped. I represented for her how Mamaw controlled her life. I get those behaviors from a long line of controllers.

I was looking forward to beginning a new life that was my own. I anticipated moving into Shelly's apartment. I would have a space that was mine, ours. My decisions would be mine to make. I was ready to take on the world. Me and Shelly. At 20 and 24 respectively, we were in this thing together. This was a beginning. I wanted to be free to engage the world on my terms. I had no idea all that day meant exactly, but I was looking to the future. I was ready as much as my sophomore in college adult experience could imagine. My world had been pretty small, but I could imagine.

The morning of the wedding day was a big moment of fear. Mamaw was still alive, and even though she liked Shelly, my marriage was the biggest challenge ever to her place of power and prominence in my life. Mom was wrapped up in her fear that she too would never live up to what she thought Mamaw wanted from her. I was hosting the biggest event of my life so far, along with Shelly, who would be another person added to this group who could be disappointed in me. As a member of one of the churches I pastored said to me, leaning in close while all robed and ready to walk down the aisle and begin worship one Sunday, "Don't screw it up." Little did he know how true that admonition rang to me.

Gavin and Marcus stayed at my parent's house the day of the rehearsal. The plan was to get up the next morning, get showered, and pack up our tuxes for the main event. The wedding was at 2:30, and we were scheduled to arrive at the church around noon. I lived a nearly 30 minute drive from the church, so we had to get on the road early enough to be on time. I did not want to be late.

We all got up and ate breakfast that morning. Showers taken. Hair put in place and removed from our faces. I was preparing last minute items that needed to go with me to the church. Then, my sense of control and planning was pulled out from under me. I noticed that Gavin and Marcus were not in the house, and their car was not in the driveway. It was dangerously close to time to leave, and I couldn't find them. There were no cell phones to call them up and say, "Where are you, and why are you messing up my day?" They were gone, and that was all I knew at that moment.

In panic, I did the only thing I could think of. I got in my car and drove around trying to find them. I drove up and down and around the country roads. I drove places that there was no reason they would be. It was like the last efforts at looking for something your child has misplaced. You start to look in places that make no sense, but there was a chance you hold on to that the favorite stuffed animal might be in the silverware drawer. That's how I was looking. I must have driven for 45 minutes to no good outcome. I went back home. Not long after, Gavin and Marcus pulled into the driveway in way too good of a mood for the harrowing experience they had just put me through.

"Where have you been? I had no idea where you were," I said with clear indignation. I was not good at hiding my frustration, or anger.

"We went to find a place to buy decorations for your 'just married' car for the reception," they answered. Clearly, I had dampened their happy mood. Smiles and laughter had turned to straight faces and tension. A few minutes later, I was driving north on Route 23, Gavin and Marcus following behind me. Finally, at last, my plans were back on track, and I was off to get married.

Shelly and I stood together in front of a full church where we had worshipped and worked together for a couple of years. The pastor wore a robe, very unlike anything this congregation had seen before, but something that I wanted for our day. I wanted to impress and dress it up a bit (all the wrong reasons for wearing robes in worship!). We used some traditional language in our vows and the words of the ceremony, the "I plight thee my troth" sort of thing. This was during the Princess Diana and Charles craze. Their wedding had taken place just two months prior. We were inspired.

I loved Shelly, and Shelly loved me, and yet, we would find out how little we knew about what that meant as the years went by, how little we knew about each other, how little about ourselves. At that moment, none of that really mattered. We had made our plans and worked hard on getting the details we wanted correct. Standing with Shelly was Lori—her maid of honor, cousin, and friend—Tammy, our mutual friend, and my sister, Ruth. With me was my friend Gavin, Shelly's brother, Brad, and a friend from my youth work at the church, Nathaniel. The men wore navy blue tuxedos with white shirts and black shoes. The women wore light blue long dresses and each carried a single white carnation. The windows were open since there was no air conditioning in the church sanctuary. It was a simple service.

We lit our unity candle, which we still have in a box (not so white as it was that day). A young couple we admired from the congregation sang the songs we had chosen. The crowd of family, friends, and coworkers of each of ours showed up. Mamaw, Papaw, Mom, and Dad were seated behind us that day watching my transition to an independent adult man, a husband. I stood at the steps in the front of a church full of people plighting my troth to a woman I revered, who was willing to spend the rest of her life with me. Thank God "for better or worse" covers a lot of stuff.

When the service was over, the organist played a song for the recessional that was not what Shelly had asked for. The organist let me know before the service started that the chosen song wouldn't happen. Unable to find the music for the original planned music, she was going to play a hymn. Since this was pretty much last minute, I said go ahead. She wondered if we should ask Shelly or just go for it. In a move that might show more of my personality than I would have thought about that day, I said, "Let's just go with it and not tell Shelly. There isn't anything to do about it anyway, so why bother her with it." It was a coup by me and the organist out of practical need.

That showed something about me that would haunt me

for decades to come, until I discovered the power of it in a therapy session with Shelly 36 years later. I was in charge. I felt like I had to protect Shelly from being hurt. Actually, it would be true of everyone in my life. I decided. Later, when I did tell her, she thought that was a fine idea and that I had made the right decision. Then again, we would also discover that Shelly didn't mind someone else protecting her from challenging moments. We were a match made in heaven, which caused us hell many times as we worked to grow and untangle our own unhealthy behavior.

No one spoke to me before the service that day. I don't mean that people didn't say hello. Many laughed, and wished me and Shelly well and much happiness. No one gave me "the talk," the "before you get married, there are some things I'd like to say to you," talk. Not even an "I'm so happy for you as you start your new life," pat on the back. Or hug.

Not my dad. Not my mom. Not my friends. Not one person.

Not "how are you doing?" Nothing.

I think it shows how superficial many of my relationships were, even with my parents. I don't know that I missed it during the flurry of activity that was my wedding day, but it is curious to me now. My dad didn't feel the need to say anything to his son. And yet, that is the way things had always been between us. My family were not exactly big huggers. Mom and Dad weren't parents who would say, "That was a great job. We are so proud of you." Or anything along those lines, including, "I love you."

I think about how many friends I had and all the people in my life, and yet they didn't really know who I was. Honestly, neither did I. I think they made assumptions about me and I about them. We just didn't talk about deep feelings or thoughts or beliefs. Hell, we didn't talk about the shallow ones either. My family got through life. We just made it through each day. Even though it covered many truths and unease, we did laugh often. We assumed what we understood as love. I carried that with me into my adult life and into my marriage. I didn't know how to be a husband. I didn't know what it meant to show up for someone or to be fully present in a moment. I knew the perfunctory actions of working, sharing money, sharing household operations, having sex, and kids, and all. However, when it came to talking and sharing on deeper levels of intimacy, not sexual intimacy, but really getting vulnerable with another person, I was clueless. I was not a vulnerability-embracing person. I held up my shield to be on guard as much as possible, since I didn't want to be vulnerable.

After a few years our children came along, born into the chaos that was my uncertainty. I didn't talk to my daughters as much as I needed to either. Being open and secure enough to have those intimate conversations about life and love and vision was difficult for a man who had to guard against abuse and manipulation and hide deepest truths about himself. I have worked hard and intentionally on myself for many years with a few different therapists. I know I'm better now than I was on that overcast but gorgeous day in 1983. Yet, still, I have to remember to say, "I love you." I have pay attention. I have to know that being vulnerable and open isn't the same as being responsible for everyone or their issues.

I married Shelly with hope for the future mixed with hope that I was proving everyone wrong, still acting out of my insecurities. I would say I didn't have the courage to be me and use my own voice to speak up, but I didn't even know who I was then. I was a compilation of what others said about me. Those statements defined me. I stood at the altar with a woman I loved, and who I still do, with a man to my right who I didn't really know very well, but who was willing to stand with me on that important day. That's the closest to acceptance I had ever come. I haven't seen or talked to Gavin since that day. I've tried to find him on social media when I think about him from time to time. I'm driven by nostalgia more than anything else though. How did he turn out? What is he doing for work? Is he married? We don't have a relationship and, really, didn't have much of one in 1983 either.

I moved back to Wilmore, Kentucky, with Shelly three years later, to attend the theological seminary (a completely unrelated institution from Asbury College, now university, except that they were across the street from each other in the same small town and bore the same name). When driving down the street one day in Wilmore, I saw a man that I thought was Marcus waiting to cross at a light. I stopped and asked out the window, "Marcus Cornell?" It was him. He got in, and we drove to a place to talk. He ended up asking me to be an usher in his wedding, which was to be in a few weeks. I did. I spent money I didn't have on my own suit, thrilled to be asked by a guy I had a connection with. I was over the top happy that a guy was giving me attention and including me in his life. I haven't seen him since his wedding. Never again was he on the street. He didn't pass on to me any word about leaving town or how to keep up our connection.

I was trying really hard to fit in with other guys. That is something I had done all of my life. I never really felt very connected to the world of the men who surrounded me growing up. I didn't like fishing. I didn't like sports. I didn't like to camp. I was no good at shooting the breeze and doing the strut your stuff act.

I was doing what you do when you're the groom at a wedding. You have someone stand with you. I had never had a man stand with me. It would be some years before I felt that closeness and connection from my own father even. Dad was part of the influencers through my early years who teased me. Mostly it was his silence that I felt enabled others to do the teasing. His silence, to me, meant in my mind there was truth to the remarks. I was different. The one time I have an actual occasion in memory that Dad teased me was just months before my wedding. He and I were in the same room. I said something about needing an umbrella for class tomorrow. He replied that he "never needed to carry an umbrella. Men don't carry umbrellas." That comment was followed by the one time I remember Mom standing up for me. She said, "And you never walked around a college campus either."

Shelly and I spent our first night as Mr. and Mrs. at the Hyatt Regency in downtown Columbus. It was the nicest hotel I had ever stayed in. We let the valet park the car, because I had never done that either. It felt so regal and important to have someone else drive our car away. I always found it curious how we will allow perfect strangers to take our cars in exchange for a small ticket with a number on it as the only proof the car existed. We entered the uber modern hotel and made our way to the lobby desk. I proudly, and in my best adult voice, asked for a reservation for Mr. and Mrs. Lykins. I made the reservation in that manner weeks prior just to have the chance to say it when the day arrived and we were really married.

After that first night, dining in the hotel restaurant, paying more for dinner than I had thought possible to charge for food, exploring the mystery and frustration at times of first attempts at physical intimacy, we were back home the next afternoon. Our presents had been delivered to our apartment (previously Shelly's apartment), and we sat down to open them. That was all by design so we could take our time and enjoy the process and recall those who had given us gifts on our special occasion. We took our time to carefully read the cards and enjoy each gift given by friends, family, and a few acquaintances. When we had completed the daunting task, I phoned home. I talked with my mom and asked if they wanted to come over and see our gifts. About 45 minutes later, my mom and dad knocked on the door. I eagerly opened it to let them enter our new-together-home on this our first full day of being husband and wife.

A few days later, we started on a trip to a place near Wilmington, Ohio. We had rented a cabin at Cowan Lake Park. This was a spot I had spent a few days as a teenager with my family in a cabin and had been impressed with the beauty of the location. Cowan was a small lake where we could lounge on a sandy beach and watch sail boats glide by. We spent a couple of days and nights, grilling steaks, hiking a couple of trails (we are not really hikers, but it seemed the thing to do in a state park), reading, and resting.

Instead of making our way home via the most direct route, I looked at the map and decided we could make a long jog and head toward Mamaw and Papaw's house. It really wasn't on the way, but I had justified it in my mind that it would be fun to stop by. There is a picture of me from our honeymoon making a call to my grandparents from a payphone. Shelly has said for years, "That's Dale calling home on our honeymoon." How prophetic that was, knowing how difficult it was for me to loosen the grip those people had on me. We drove along curvy roads for what seemed like way too long in a car on our honeymoon week. The weather was perfect. The sun was bright. The September sky was blue. At least it was a good day for a drive.

We ended up in Beaver, after a couple of hours and 80 rural miles. We ate dinner with them and made our way back to Columbus, another hour and a half drive and another 80 miles. As we left Beaver, we drove north toward Columbus, to start a new life, just like my mom and dad had done in 1962. We even traveled the same road. A gorgeous sunny day was ending, and I was feeling better having made sure everyone was okay.

I look back on that moment and wonder what it was all about. It is intriguing to me that I was focused on my family members and paying them homage during that important week in my life as a newly married man. It was the beginning of a new life that was about me and my wife and the two of us as family. I know that doesn't exclude the involvement and addition of other family members, but during that week? What was going on inside of me?

Mamaw had done such a thorough job of manipulating me to feel responsible for her well-being that I was driven to take my wife during our honeymoon to visit her and check in. I had such a need to connect with her, the woman who had been the most important person to me so far.

Notice we didn't stop at Shelly's family home and see her parents. It was about me. I was the one who hadn't made the separation that would enable me to move forward on my own. It would be many years before I finally was able to sort through the moments and forces that made those unhealthy relationships. Mamaw, for instance, was a woman who had latched onto my life and blurred her reality with my own reality. I was unable to be me. I had no idea who I was apart from Mamaw. Her influence on me remained strong for a long time after. Shelly would compete with that on some level for years to come.

The following week, I ended up calling home in tears from our apartment. At the time, I justified it by saying I was homesick. At the moment I was both surprised by that and at the same time decided to own it. Shelly was understanding. Shelly is always understanding. She understood what it was like for life to change and how difficult it was to give way to new unknowns. She knew when she moved into that apartment two years before that once in a while you miss home and the familiar people and surroundings. For both of us, that was true in spite of those people and surroundings triggering negative memories on several occasions. Still, there were happy memories too.

Twenty-Four

UNBOUND

When I was 21, Mamaw went to the hospital for back pain that had become more than she could bear. Her pain was bad enough that plans had been made to move her and Papaw into my mom and dad's house where they could be cared for by mom in anticipation of their deteriorating health down the road. For Mamaw that road was a short cul-de-sac. She ended up at the hospital in Chillicothe before any further plans were formalized. I visited as often as I could while attending my classes at Ohio State and living with Shelly in Columbus. As I was leaving one evening, Mamaw sat on the edge of the hospital bed facing the opposite direction toward the window, her back to me while I stood at the door. "What is wrong with me?" she asked of no one in particular. It was really a cry for answers to the pain that had now overtaken her world. If I thought her world was quite small before, now it was even smaller, a hospital room that would yield to her bedroom. That was the last place she ever was. The question, along with the image of the woman who was so influential in my life, was devastating to me. I drove home that night in tears. I knew the end of an era was coming and I wasn't sure what that meant for me.

The doctors completed an exploratory surgery, since they could get no definitive answers to the very question Mamaw asked that evening. Soon into the start of the surgery, they found cancer all over her body. They discovered a tumor in her breast that was likely the beginning of it all. The doctors asked if she knew it was there. She said yes. When asked how long ago she had noticed it, she answered, "Seven years." There was nothing to do then but send her home. And we all knew that home was where she wanted to spend the last weeks of her life.

Mamaw lay in the same room that had been hers for decades, now in a hospital bed. Friends and family were nearly always in the house in those last days. My mom moved into the house, taking up residence in her childhood room. A group of women sang hymns and songs like that in the style of music familiar and common in the church of our family roots in eastern Kentucky—just voices that droned out a haunting melody. Women and men came by to hold Bible study, pray, and even preach while Mamaw lay in the adjoining room.

During one visit to the house, in one of Mamaw's lucid moments, she had me lean in close to her mouth as she said as quietly as possible, "There's some money for you in the bedroom. You know where to find it." Even though glad for the news, I was surprised she thought of telling me in the state she was in. She wasn't always able to interact with what was going on around her, but she was aware enough this day to remember there had been money in the secret depository. She always thought of me.

Shelly, Ruth, and I, along with others who had stayed the night knowing death was near, had slept anywhere we could in the small house. I was on the kitchen floor on blankets and old handmade quilts with several others. At least it was carpeted. We were awakened about 2:30 am. She was nearly gone. I joined others in her room as we stood around her bed. She quit breathing and slipped away from us. It was beautiful and terrifying all at once. Anxiety rose from deep within my body. My teeth started chattering as if I were cold, even though it was not winter. At first it startled me, and then I realized I was extremely stressed. The chattering didn't stop for several minutes. This person who so engulfed my life for the sake of her own wellbeing was gone.

The undertaker from the local funeral home came to remove Mamaw's body from the house she had called home for over 30 years. Cheryl, the woman who owned the funeral home, was so kind. It was Versa Jenkins after all. After the decades of living in the very same place and interacting with the same people, Mamaw was well known and liked. Cheryl comforted us with her soft gentle manner and peaceful words. As my teeth chattered, I watched Mamaw's body be removed. I realized I had never lost any family member this close to me to death before. It was a big deal. Mamaw's absence was a big deal. I could not help her be okay any longer.

Shortly after her death, I was told there was one bank account that had my name and Mamaw's on it jointly. I never knew about that account. Since I was on the account and not my grandfather, I had to go to the bank to close it out. It had about $5,000 in it saved from Mamaw's Social Security checks and from selling her quilts. That's the only way I knew of that she earned money. I took it. I thought about sharing it with my sister. There was no surprise nest egg Mamaw left for her. But, I did not. Even in death, Mamaw made sure I had a connection to her. She called it love.

"Blessed Savior there to guide us till we reach that blissful shore and the angels there to join us in God's grace forevermore." Grace—something Mamaw didn't know much about in her life and something she didn't extend to many. I don't mean the divine kind. That's given to us all whether we realize it as such or not. I mean the human kind, that allows others to grow and flourish into who they were meant to be. Mamaw's life was wrapped up in those walls on Beaver Pike, in a man who was never really her lover, and in a family she controlled.

She left us all behind in her wake to fend for ourselves and find out how truly dependent we had become. Twenty years later, I made the discovery that Mamaw, for all of her presence and influence in my life, was not the best thing that ever happened to me. I had always thought she was. Even though as a young boy she abused me, that reality had been overshadowed by her manipulation. My personal desires were wrapped up in hers. She wanted to be sure I felt responsible for her. I'm not sure if my anxiety that night stemmed from feeling alone or free. It would be years before I delved into the depths of the pathology she unleashed in me. I still am uncovering layers of it to this day. But in that moment, on some primal level, I knew that a seismic shift had taken place in my life and in our family. I would never be the same. That was good, eventually.

A few years after Mamaw's death, Papaw died of prostate cancer. He had lived with prostate troubles as long as I can remember. It was as an occasional topic of conversation in the house. Mamaw and Papaw would discuss how he had to get up and "make water," as he called it, through the night. He had at least one surgery on his prostate gland. On that occasion, we spent hours at the hospital. Those were the days when you stayed in the hospital for at least a week, if not weeks, after a surgery. If it wasn't two weeks, it felt like it. I was a young teen boy who had other things to do. But, we would visit and stay and greet and entertain the family who came by in droves. His room was so full of people someone would have to step out before someone else could go in. He came from a large family of nine siblings accompanied by assorted nieces and nephews. I don't know if they came because of affection for Papaw or just because his surgically required hospital stay provided a place for them to go. It was something to do.

I was unsure how to feel as I stood at his casket. Before me lay the body of Luster Jenkins—the man who had caused me so much pain. I would not even understand the depth of it until many years later. I stood over his lifeless body feeling mostly numb. My mom was busy with details, but I knew she was hiding her true feelings and emotions, something she had become good at over the years.

Only three weeks later, Papaw's son, Buford, died as well. Buford was a man I always thought of as sad. He was divorced and lived alone. His house was close to Mamaw and Papaw's farm. For many years, he was just a country version of next door. You could see his house across the garden and the adjacent field from the back porch. You could at least tell when the lights were on at night. Noting whether Buford was home or not occupied the time of Mamaw and Papaw who would say, "Buford isn't home; his light is off." I didn't understand why any of us really cared, but they did, Papaw more than Mamaw actually. Mamaw had deep negative opinions about Buford. She would get upset when he came to visit, never letting him see or know that, of course. Once she saw him walking up her driveway and said, "Oh my God, here comes the biggest plague that ever walked the earth." I still smile at the thought of her controlled boldness.

I don't know where that attitude grew from. Buford was

Papaw's son by his second wife. He and Mamaw never had children of their own. Buford was Mom's biological father. Did that have anything to do with it? Was Buford one of the few people who knew the truth and could topple the stories that had been told to hide the truth? I am not sure, but whatever it was, Mamaw didn't like Buford.

Mom had told me stories about Papaw being really strict with her when she was growing up in his house. For instance, as a teen, he would drop her off at the Jolly Spot, the local teen hangout burger place with a jukebox. On Saturday nights, especially, it was the place to be in rural Pike County, Ohio. There wasn't much else to do. He would come back promptly at nine o'clock to pick her up. She was mortified and upset, since that was the time most people were just arriving, and things were hopping.

Even though Mom had cared for him in her home during the last months of his life, she had a deep sense of guilt and anger co-mingled inside. Not dealing with any of those emotions had kept her closed off from herself for her entire life. That anger came out in inappropriate ways and was directed at people who were more convenient than they were suitable targets. Papaw was the face and person behind it all. Buford may have been too. When she was 17, she had been told that Buford, passed off as a half-brother, was her biological father. At least, that was the story. There had been some questioning of it over the decades that followed the reveal, but no one ever corroborated another story. Was Luster the real biological father of Mom, and Buford took the fall for the old man? We may never know the answer to that riddle.

Luster kept a tight watch on my mom. Being the janitor at the school she attended made it much easier for him to know everything about her day, including whether she was sneaking off at lunch to look at the dead bodies in their finest clothes and hair styles in the window of the Cox Funeral Home. Yes, that was a thing. I said there wasn't much to do.

When Buford died, she was distressed. I stayed with her the night before the funeral. Following the visitation, Mom was in tears. She expressed her negative feelings and thoughts about these two men. I encouraged her to just let it out and be honest with herself.

The next day we stood at the casket of Buford, and I said to Mom, "This is the last person in the deceitful story of your birth and life that caused you so much pain. Let it all go with him to the grave and release it and all of the perpetrators of the lie. They will not have a grip on you any longer."

I don't know if she ever did that. We have never talked about it since. Once I came to terms with my memories of abuse at the hands of Papaw, she expressed her anger at him, even 30 years after his death. It brought it all back as she remembered how much destruction he had caused.

I stood at Papaw's casket before his funeral and was kind of glad that this chapter was all over. Yet, the effects of the actions and lack of ability to show love in healthy ways, the silence, and the lies followed me around long after. They were still part of other people's lives too, many more than I even knew at the moment. Other boys who were victims, other family members, like my mom, who were caught in his part of a destructive story line.

Years later, I was able to stand at the grave of Mamaw and Papaw and let them know I had found the truth. I knew more than they ever wanted me to know. They had hurt me for the last time. I forgave them, and in that act of forgiveness, I was taking my life back. It took time. I had to face the reality of my experiences with them. In that process, the wounds in me healed, even if their effects still influence my own fear, struggles, behavior, and worries at times. In forgiving, I don't condone or dismiss. I let go of how those experiences define me or control me. They were both dead by the time I dealt with any of this. If they had been alive, I'm sure I would not have kept them in my life.

Mamaw and Papaw did terrible things. Yet, somewhere in them, even though deeply hidden, was the image of a Creator who values every person in the mess that is our human condition. If only each of us knew how much potential for wholeness and love is just beneath the surface.

Twenty-Five

LEARNING & UNLEARNING

I had been through an incredible personal journey through voice therapy, counseling, and singing lessons. Each of those disciplines helped me discover layers to my life and experiences that were transformative. Each of them had contributed to a healing journey discovering how much stress I held in my body that was actually causing harm to me physically. I was cowering. It was time to build on what I had started—what God had started. My professional life was the next layer to examine. I made the decision to take what is called a Renewal Leave in the United Methodist Church. Every six years, clergy are entitled to take up to six months paid Leave. This would be the first time I had ever taken one in 28 years. Once I made the decision, I knew it was right.

The Church Board approved the five weeks off I asked for. During April and early May in 2018, I walked away from the daily responsibilities of my work and stepped into a time to breathe. It was glorious. I made myself stay home and didn't even get dressed the first day. I had to make my body and mind understand this was not business as usual. I rested, napped, read, watched television, and rested some more while unwinding from the hamster wheel that was my life. I made plans to visit friends and mentors of mine across the country. All in all, I was in an airplane six times over the five weeks and took one shorter trip in a car. I spaced out the dates so that I had time between to rest again. I found myself walking slower and noticing things around me, including the people I encountered. I am always on the fast-track when I am moving. I walk fast. I drive fast. I live fast. So, it was refreshing and ground-breaking for me to walk at a slower pace. It was nice to have few time constraints. There was no need to hurry when running errands (yes, they still needed done, but they became the day's goals not intrusions). No need to rush to get to the next place. It would wait, and I would get there when I got there.

I read books that I had chosen to help focus my discernment of my own personal goals as I determined what was important to me. I asked questions while I read and paid attention to what I felt God was trying to say to me in that moment through the authors' words. It was good to catch up with friends. One couple I visited I hadn't seen for ten years, although the husband, Matt, and I had been great friends nearly 30 years before. You may have experienced that feeling of picking right up where you left off even though time had marched on. That's the gift that was mine during those three days.

Matt told me about a section of stories of Jesus' life in John Chapter 6. It includes hard teachings where it seems as if Jesus is trying to make it really difficult for people, as Matt put it, to run them away from following him. The disciples found Jesus on the other side of a lake and asked, "Rabbi, when did you get here?" Jesus replied, "You are looking for me because I fed you with those loaves of bread and many fish. You are chasing the miracles. You don't really want to do the hard work that I am asking." The story continues with Jesus basically telling them that their religious heritage and ancestry won't count for anything in the end. The Bible says that many of his followers left him. They walked away. Jesus' closest 12 disciples grumbled among themselves about all of this, and he asked, "You don't want to leave too do you?"

Matt was helping me see that Jesus himself was pretty disruptive and upset people by some things he said. He challenged the assumptions people made and asked them to go beyond their comfort level and what they knew and expected. People left him. They stopped following him. Why would I expect anything different? People are the same now as they were in Jesus' day.

Why was I so afraid of people deciding that following Jesus was not what they wanted? Jesus didn't even sweat over those decisions. He didn't feel rejected. He just told people how hard it would be, and let them decide. He respected their decision. Not everyone ran away. Some wished they had done so later! Everyone is free to decide, and that's a God-given gift. Speak the truth, and let it stand on its own merit. Since I had been carrying around shame and had been manipulated by abuse, I was always trying to prove something. I tried to prove my worth. I tried to prove my right to even exist. I felt I was an intrusion. That was my challenge at times. I was also afraid of people walking away. Worship attendance would go down. Money would drop off. The way I saw it, the decision to walk away would have been a judgement on me. The denominational church acted as if that were true.

There is a trap that modern Christianity perpetuates continually. The institution needs people and money to survive. Too often, churches make decisions or structure "ministry" around what will attract the most people and money for the survival of the church itself. I knew that approach had little to do with Jesus. However, it was all I had known or been taught. Five years before this, I had attempted to organize church differently based on some new experiences being taught and shared that were less centralized and more outward focused, but it was not an easy path.

I invited 25 people to my house one evening for ice cream and conversation. Myself and the associate pastor at the time shared our burden and enthusiasm for doing church differently. We asked them to be part of a summer long experiment. We would organize ourselves into two groups who would meet in our homes. During those gatherings we would study and pray together. Then one week each month, we reached out to connect with an actual neighbor in our lives, maybe on the street where we lived. Another week of the month, we would reach out in service stretching beyond our comfort level to meet a need, as a group. We believed we were church, as real and powerful as the bigger institution. Actually, we thought we could be more authentic than the wider formalized church could ever be.

Out of that summer came a variety of groups that multiplied to continue the same experiment. Some lasted longer than others, but I was part of leading a community like that for years. I was committed to changing the way church was thought about and defined, as well as lived.

At the larger church I pastored, we were making progress in moving in that direction for the entire organization. The conviction that our faith was not wrapped up in an institution and could be more organic in the local places God was already at work became the core of how the leaders of that congregation saw its purpose. After the associate pastor who led us in this direction left, we hired a staff person to continue in this effort, and we kept going.

It was difficult to shift an organized traditional church to this model. I found out that people only knew their experience of what church had always been for them. That was true for some of them for decades. It was threatening to some. Others felt as if they were judged for what they had been doing for years. That was never how I wanted anyone to feel and fed into my personal fears. Still, the transition was rocky. Nothing in the denominational structure supported it or understood it, let alone the people in the pews. They had been conditioned by the consumer culture the church has embodied and championed to keep the money coming.

My mentors encouraged me and challenged me to keep embracing change. During my Renewal Leave, my coach said she wanted me to make a list of things I would stop. Adding, "and, I hope it's a long one."

Here's the List:

- Responding to others' sense of urgency
- Measuring my worth by whether my church paid its dues to the denomination
- Checking worship attendance weekly
- Allowing a certain staff person to set the agenda for the church
- Giving people a pass on clearly defined expectations
- Judging myself
- Bypassing/avoiding difficult conversations
- Giving away my power
- Being fuzzy. State my yes and no
- Focusing on the end result
- Tolerating any gray-area regarding all being welcome in the church

- Preaching as the sage on the stage
- Making/perpetuating consumer Christians
- Worrying about money and resources
- Attending denominational events that I don't feel fit my passion or goals
- Spending my time on the business of the institution of the church
- Believing the institution has any power over me
- Using canned confirmation curriculum
- Holding membership classes

She also suggested I create an exit plan that would allow me to leave the United Methodist Church. She said, "You may never use it, but you need to have the peace that comes with knowing you have a plan if you ever need it." She said that brought freedom to go all-in and let the chips fall where they may in speaking truth and sharing my own values and ideas.

One mentor said I needed the clout of experience behind my teaching and influence. If I wanted the church to be different, then I had to actively do what I said. He was referring to my passion that had ignited five years prior about living faith every day outside the walls and confines of the church building. I was turned off by the idea that was prevalent in the Church in most places that set up an us-versus-them mentality—the notion that the church has to attract people outside the church to come to the building to hear about Jesus. I thought, with the changing culture surrounding us, that was an increasingly ineffective strategy. I was drawn to the idea that God is already at work in every location and in every person in the world. So, we followers of Jesus need to join what God is already doing. Out there. And, not for the sake of building up the institutional church itself, but for the sake of God's reign or Kingdom or justice to be announced. That was way more exciting than filling seats on Sundays to watch a show, give money, leave, and wait to do it all again. I don't remember Jesus ever saying anything like that.

So, I started writing a blog, "Unlearning Church." Through it, I shared stories and thoughts I had about how to unlearn the old ways of church for living a new fresh relevant life. One book I read during that Leave time, *Walking with Nehemiah* by Joseph W. Daniels, asked what was my passion. I had realized I had no idea. So, I spent time that day reflecting on that question. I identified that it was connecting with people who have been lied to by the church. In other words, people who have been told that getting involved in church activity, giving money, and showing up once in a while were the things that comprised actually following the teachings of Jesus. I was passionate about bringing healing and connection to people who have experienced exclusion from the church. I wanted to be part of an authentic community where people were real and honest about their questions, struggles, and lives. I wanted to celebrate a big table where a diverse group of folks was welcome.

The last week of my Renewal Leave I spent with my wife, Shelly, in Naples, Florida. The beach has always been a place for me of spiritual connection. Nothing helps me feel small in context of the big wide world better than the ocean. The smallness I refer to is not negative or self-deprecating. It has to do with feeling that I'm part of something much larger than myself. That brings me relaxing peace and contentment. I can sit for a long time just watching the waves roll in and out. I can just listen to the sounds of the ocean and the beach.

A trip to Virginia Beach, the first one my wife and I ever

took without any kids, turned out to be one of my favorite beach moments. We were alone for a week with no schedule. We woke up in the morning when we wanted to. Most often the morning involved putting on some swim trunks and a button up shirt, throwing on a pair of flip flops and walking with Shelly on the sandy beach. The morning sun was beginning its journey into a new day, just like us, as it shone over the Atlantic to the east. Shelly and I set up camp in the sand. Beach chairs, umbrella, towels, sunscreen, hats, sunglasses, all part of our survival supplies. And, a book each. I opened my book, which I had been anticipating reading, but then I closed it as quickly as I had opened it. I just sat there taking in that moment in my life. I wanted nothing else. I never did read that year while on the beach. I reserved that for in the room later in the evenings and before bed. On the beach that year, I realized I didn't want to leave my feeling of total contentment to enter the world of the author. As amazing as the book was, it didn't compare to what was right in front of me and all around, surrounding me with awareness of life.

It is still hard for me to read on the beach, even though I always take a book just in case I can't help myself. The beach, the ocean specifically, but any waterside spot really, is a place of remembering for me. I am reminded that my life ebbs and flows. I am reminded that life on this planet has followed that same pattern for as long as it has been. The sun starts in the east and follows its path to the west every day. The birds fight for scraps of food flapping in place against the wind to wait out their human benefactors. I am reminded that my life is like that, caught in the rhythm of something far larger than what I can think about most days.

I returned home with a few more days to rest before

entering the world of work again on Monday. I was actually looking forward to returning, although, I will admit, I wished at times I had taken advantage of the additional weeks or months I could have taken. I was not looking forward to returning to my seagull-like flapping that had become a part of how I had approached my work. However, over those weeks I had begun to see, even if just a sliver of an amount on the horizon, that there could be another way to exist.

To mark what I was feeling was the beginning of a new era in my life, I redecorated my office the last weekend. I had ordered new artwork and got it hung on the wall. It was much more modern in style than the icons and pictures I had placed on my walls for decades. I bought new lamps that were also more modern. Like Easter Sunday, I bought new clothes to mark the occasion and symbolize new life (at least that's what we tell ourselves regarding Easter purchases, and I didn't mind using the same line of excuse).

I also had commissioned an artist in the congregation to paint a picture of me and Jesus laughing while on the beach. All of my life, when I have felt God nearest me, I have expressed that awareness through laughter. I certainly don't control it. It just bubbles up from deep inside me and comes out as pure joy. I feel my experiences of awareness of God are moments of clarity for me personally of a reality that is already so. I acknowledge God in my life and made an intentional decision to bend my life's energy toward God's purposes in the world. This laughter sometimes surprises me. I am not always expecting it to happen when it does. I may be going through a very difficult moment, one that is stretching on for days or weeks, and I pray and in the middle of that moment when I am intentionally listening and aware of God, I laugh. It is as if God helps me see there is hope and that what I think is never-ending will indeed pass and that I am okay in the midst until it does.

My Spiritual Director asked me one day, "What are you and Jesus going to do this day?" I said, "Go to a beach and laugh." She indicated she'd love to see that image. I realized I could make that happen, since I would actually like to see it too. And, there you have the beginning of the oil painting that now hangs in my office space. I admit, it does often take some explaining. Not many people have a painted portrait of themselves and Jesus, let alone one in which they are laughing like buddies hanging out at the beach—him in a robe and me in a Nautica shirt.

It felt great to have taken the time to do the hard work the Renewal Leave afforded me. I was refreshed. I was ready to get back. I was more authentically myself. I was going to lead us where we had said we were going as a church. I had a plan to get out if the denominational system continued to get sicker instead of healthier. Those five weeks showed me that there was more to life than this one experience I had lived for nearly 30 years. Even though it wasn't all bad, it had become increasingly out of sync with my own journey.

Before my Leave, I felt like I had to quiet my own feelings and thoughts. Preaching had become a bit rote. I avoided tough topics so as not to upset the financial base. If I told people the truth, they might just leave. People, Christians, aren't necessarily into the truth. Preaching what Jesus taught by his life example would freak out most Christians who claim to follow him. We tend to sanitize it all. How do those two things square? They don't, but we can't tell the truth, or churches would be empty.

From what the Bible actually tells us, that's what Jesus would do if he were here walking around right now. He'd be okay with empty church buildings. He would trade them for people who are loving. He would rather have justice for the outsider than full church buildings. Like the WWJD bracelets that were popular a few years ago, "What would Jesus do if he were here?" He would run us all out of the places of honor we create for ourselves and replace us with the least among the world's people. He would seat the marginalized at the table. Wouldn't that piss off the people who thought they were doing the righteous thing?

I was in this moment in life when I knew I had to make some major changes. I had to speak truth. I had to name reality. I needed to say what I believed. Certainly, I still wanted to do all of that in ways that aided in people hearing what I had to share rather than being instantly polarized and shut off. Nevertheless, truth must be told. I accepted that I was called and sent to share my ideas. I had been placed where I was in order to be an influence. Influencing comes with certain positions, and I was in one. That's how things were designed, and I would say that's how God wanted them. In other words, I owned that God called me with a unique voice and my own ideas. Up until my Renewal Leave, I had been always seeking out other people's ideas and stories. Now, I wanted to just share who I was and what I thought as well.

The first week back, a staff member asked me a question, and I gave her an answer right away. It was clear, and I knew what I thought. I didn't have to ask her what she thought. After all, she was asking for my input. So, I gave it to her. She was surprised and immediately noticed. She even said something affirming that change. Of course, that wasn't always the reaction. There were some leaders and staff who were invested in my acquiescence.

I realized that there were people who were in the wrong

seats on the bus, so to speak. There were others who shouldn't have been on the bus at all. My inability to say with clarity what was best for the whole organization and everyone in it had led to uncertainty. That uncertainty manifested itself in sluggish movement and taking paths that weren't getting to the destination. Then again, I don't think everyone was aware of the end place we were heading toward.

In the pulpit, I became bolder in my preaching. I named the shortfalls of an institutional form of religion that had been passed off as following Jesus for far too long. I called out our lack of inclusive spirit, especially where LGBTQ+ people were concerned. I preached on community. I preached on diversity. I connected the principals of acceptance and love and grace to Jesus's teachings found in the New Testament Gospels.

We started to reorganize structures around our decentralized missional goals. Out in the neighborhoods is where I wanted people to spend most of their time. That's where people were who needed to know that they were loved beyond imagination by God and by other human beings. We all need to hear that, but those of us who were on the inside of that congregation should have heard it many times. It was time to share it and put feet to our prayers.

Man, this caused a fight with one staff member who was used to being the one making the charts and setting the categories. She was used to having her way. It was extremely difficult for her to let me have that role, even though it should've been mine all along. I had allowed her to have undue and unbalanced, even unchecked, influence for far too long. I stood up to her. I was her boss after all. I started saying no when her ideas were contrary to mine and the direction the Board had cast for us all. I'm not going to get into the gory details, but I will say it was a show down. It was a situation that needed correcting, as difficult as that was.

There is a place in the Bible where it is written, "Let your yes be yes and your no be no." Most people interpret that to mean that you should stand for what you believe and stick with your convictions. That is one way of understanding what I had found in myself. The ability to speak a clear yes when needed, as well as being able to say a clear and definitive no when needed, was part of my newfound confidence. All my life I have felt like my voice didn't matter. It was as if I were trying to get someone's attention. I just wanted someone to hear me. I wanted someone to care about me. I needed to matter.

Once my Renewal Leave was over, I went to counseling again and did even more work through the years of child sexual abuse I experienced. I worked on understanding who I was and what was important to me. I decided what I believed and trusted that to anchor my life. I truly was a more passionate and purposeful person. I brought that clarity to my work as a pastor. I knew what I wanted to do with my energy and the rest of my life. I would not be part of expanding the institutional church any longer. My priority was in the missional movement that took the church out of the buildings and to where people are. I was going to be honest and open about my conviction that the church, however organized, should be affirming and open to all people, especially LGBTQ+ people.

I also knew that I would live my passion, whether in the United Methodist Church or not. So, I made that exit plan, just in case.

I needed it about a year later, when it became clear that the United Methodist Church, which I fell in love with 30 years prior, was no longer the same church. Institutional survival had become the main point. That did not fit my values, so I undid my shackles and I left.

Twenty-Six

COMING OUT

My dad was emotionally absent until I was 22 and had my own child. Something happened to him at that time. When I was a boy and a teen, I remember Dad spending most all of his time outside. I believe he was avoiding the constant threat of confrontation that loomed from my mom. Like a storm perpetually brewing, he never knew when it would strike. It could be a blast of power and wind or a silent shut-down and shut-out. Either way, it was never predictable. That was what my dad was avoiding. Unfortunately, his avoidance shut him out of my life too. The two of us could be together and never speak a word.

But, when my first child was born, Dad was present. He was working in the town we lived in and would stay with us at night, arriving about dinnertime each day. He was wonderful. We talked. We engaged. It is like he saw me and acknowledged me. That was never easy. I understand that more now than I did then of course. He was raised by parents who were not emotionally connected. He was lost in a sea of seven other siblings. My dad was the one who dropped out of school and worked at the family business.

Neither of my parents had role models of healthy relationships. Of course, how many of us really do, and are there such things? They were both starved for attention from those who were supposed to love them and protect them. Instead, those were the very people who were abusive and dismissive. They passed on their hurt and unsettled needs to the next generation. As much as I wanted to avoid doing that with my own daughters, I know I have not succeeded. All I can hope for is that they were given more than I was, and they will do more than I have for the next generation.

Then there is my wife. She is the exception in my life. Another human being herself who was raised in an unsupportive household. That is putting it mildly. She had a mother who was wrapped up in herself. Her mom wore the anger of years of her own misery on her face and shared it through her voice. Her dad was mentally ill, blaming everyone else for his situation in life. He was forced to retire early due to his depression, and he spiraled downward into an even worse clinical depression that never lifted. His depression silenced the joy of the other family members. It choked life out of the household. Shelly had a brother she fought with all the time. Fear of abandonment was always present. Fear of never being good enough was drilled into every report card day. "Well, that's good, but it could be better," was her dad's answer to most everything. In spite of all of those challenges, Shelly is the one who actually showed me unconditional love for the first time in my life. I have certainly tested that over these many years, but she has been steadfast.

It is a wonder that we have stayed together through the thick and thin of life's journey. We made a commitment, and we really love each other. Those are two strong ties that bind. We love our family and the life we have created. So, we keep going through all the moments when we thought, "Fuck, here we go, again!" It is to this binding that I attribute Shelly's response when, after 35 years of marriage, two kids, two grandchildren, and several pets, I told her I was gay.

I was laying on the couch with my head propped up and my legs stretched out, the television in front of me. I had no idea that this movie I had seen previewed in the theater, which I was now watching at home, would change my life. All of my questions and wrestling would end in an hour and 50 minutes.

I had wanted to see "Love, Simon" since we saw that preview months earlier. When it showed up on our Netflix DVD list, I moved it to our queue, and it had arrived in the mail. Yes, this was 2018, but we had gotten DVDs from Netflix since the beginning of the service, which was revolutionary those many years ago. By 2018, it just elicited response of, "I didn't know they still did that." But, we kept getting the mailed red envelopes that were nice gifts of entertainment opportunities appearing in our mailbox.

I watched the film as Simon, a high school senior, looked out his second floor bedroom window as a landscaping truck pulled up across the street. A young man opened the truck door, one muscular leg was revealed as his booted foot made contact with the pavement beneath. Then the rest of his gorgeous body was revealed as he exited the truck and prepared for his work.

Simon noticed, and I noticed. I was right there with the main character. Even before it was obvious that the scene was going to play out that way, my mind went there. The guy's leg was the first thing I noticed. I was drawn to this figure on the screen representing all the other guys before him who I had noticed in the same way. I was drawn to him. I wasn't surprised. This reaction was very common. I always noticed.

I looked. I always was very aware of male presence. Drawn to the masculinity of their physical features.

I longed to feel connected, hoping to believe I was like any one of them and that they would welcome me into the fraternity of maleness. I was tormented by the desire but relegated to looking. This was my struggle. It had been mine from my earliest memories—silently bearing the weight of it. Except for one person and a few counselors, I hadn't ever spoken of it. That one person had been Shelly, my wife, who was sitting in her chair next to the couch watching the movie with me on our annual vacation in July.

The scene with the man and the truck was one of the very first in the movie. The tale unfolded of Simon, who wrestled with telling his friends and family that he was gay but who was outed by a classmate and forced to reveal his truth. "You get to be more you than you have ever been," his mother said to him at one moment of upheaval. Simon didn't want his life to change. He feared the changes that would come his way if he was honest. He dreaded the awkwardness that would be placed on his friendships and how people would act differently once they learned who the real Simon was, who he had hidden from the world.

When the movie ended, Simon was happy (I'll let you discover for yourself how he gets there), and I was in tears. I knew at that moment I had to admit my truth. I was gay. For 55 years I had lived with a struggle. That is how I referred to my feelings and attractions. I had believed—had been sure— that, if I just could work through the struggle with a therapist, it would be "healed." If I could just get enough male friends or replace the male bonding I never had growing up, I would be "normal." If I just prayed enough or showed God I was serious about changing who I was to meet the expectations of the world and the church and, even I thought, the Bible, I would struggle no more.

On that day, in that moment, having watched that movie, I knew better. I just knew. I felt as if God had sat right down next to me and said, "Give up the struggle. Admit it. You are gay."

It was no longer acceptable to deny this reality that had been my companion since early childhood. I had no idea what was going to happen, but I knew I had to speak it out loud. I asked Shelly to have a seat beside me on the couch. She could tell I had been crying.

"I don't know how to say this or where to start," I said nervously, knowing my life was about to change. I also knew, which may be the most fearful aspect, that Shelly's life was about to change.

Shelly looked at me and said, "So, you really are gay, aren't you?"

"Yes," I said, tears bursting through again at the sound of truth piercing the air of denial.

She knew about my self-defined struggle. I had shared it with her over the years, and together, we hoped it would go away in time. Relegated to a box that could be looked at and worked on, it didn't seem to have so much power. Sitting there with her, though, the box was thrown out and truth was sitting right there on the floor in front of us, which was much scarier.

We talked and decided right then that neither of us had any desire to disrupt our lives by separation. We loved each other. We loved our family. We enjoyed the life we had built. We didn't know what the future would bring, but we knew that we had the time and the commitment to figure it out.

I had never been more relieved. In the next couple of

days, I went to a bookstore, made my way to the magazine section, and with boldness and no hiding picked up a copy of "Out" magazine. I didn't know where else to start. I purchased it, placing it on the counter, mustering all the courage inside to tell myself, this is me, and there is no need to hide it.

And yet, there was still hiding to be done. At the time, I was the pastor of a church that would not be affirming. Coming out as gay could have professional consequences. I could even lose my ministry and ordination. Shelly and I kept this new reality close to us for months. We wanted to live with it for some time and figure out what impact it would have on our lives. What does this really mean? How will it really work? We did tell a friend who was also gay and who worked in the mental health field, because we knew we could trust him and that he would be helpful and encouraging to us.

On Mother's Day weekend, 2019, nine months later, I told my kids. Their response was, "Duh. We've known that for a long time." Apparently, it was said about me among their friends that their dad was either "gay or the gayest straight man ever." That response was shared by many I came out to over the next months. Actually, it always made me feel affirmed to know that others saw it before me. There was something encouraging about those relationships.

Shelly and I admitted to our kids that the previous few months had been very difficult at times. Shelly was dealing with years of fear of being left out, insecurities, and denying her feelings. My coming out and the relationship we would need to build after was the catalyst for all of those issues screeching into consciousness for her. She started her own therapy, and we held on for the journey.

That same Mother's Day weekend, I told my mother her son was gay. She was visiting for the holiday, and I took her to the basement family room where we could have some privacy. I let her know that I had told Shelly that I was gay. I told her I had always been gay but was just now finding the courage and support to admit it to myself and a few others. She said good things. She still loved me she assured me. Her biggest concern was my soul and what she had been taught the Bible says against homosexuals. I told her some of my own understanding of the Bible itself and the importance of cultural and contextual interpretation of the Bible, which when applied to those few passages that seem to condemn homosexuality showed it may not be the case after all.

I told Dad and his wife and the response was, "You're still family and we (him and my stepmom) still love you." We have never spoken of it again since.

That's where most of my family lands. We just never speak of it. I bring it up occasionally but feel like it isn't met with the desire to hear any more. Really, I am not judging them. I understand it's difficult to change, but I would love for someone to say, "How are you doing?" rather than never saying anything and what then feels to me like attempting to ignore it.

During the months after my initial conversation with Shelly, she and I did some research looking for support that might be available in the LGBTQ+ community. That caused us to discover that our decision to remain married had a name and that there were others who were attempting it. We are in what is called a mixed orientation marriage. The only way we could ever consider such a life is due to the foundation of our love. It is our commitment and love that keeps us together in the difficult times and helps us persevere when we are facing our own demons. That is our biggest discovery. Any issues we have had over this mixed orientation marriage stems from individual issues we have carried with us all of our lives. The hard parts have been doing the work on ourselves and then bringing that change in each of us individually to our relationship together. Up to this moment, we had been used to the comfort of our marriage. Shelly has invited me to explore what being gay means for me. Her love for me wants me to know the fulfillment of being a gay man. That gift has been so healing for me and drawn me closer emotionally to her.

Not long after coming out to myself and Shelly, the denomination of the United Methodist Church, in which I was ordained and had been a pastor during the previous 30 years, made decisions that further alienated LGBTQ+ people and their allies. It was one reason I decided to leave the denomination and strike out on another life. I wanted to live a life that was fully honest about my belief that all people are to be included in the church. I refer to it as being openly open and affirming. In other words, that Church was not aligning with my beliefs any longer.

That gay friend Shelly and I had told about my orientation texted me after I told him I would leave the United Methodist Church and said, "We could always start an open affirming church in the area." He offered a space to meet in and a house for us to live in while we settled and moved into a new phase of life, both of which made it obvious that what he proposed was possible. I agreed, and we began to write out our ideas of what this new community of faith would look like.

We were going to be focused on the mission and not the institution. We also knew, first and foremost, that it would be unapologetically open to LGBTQ+ folks and provide a safe space.

We launched The Open Table in July 2019, with about 50 people. We had met together for nearly six months when the time came that I wanted to be able to be honest with the whole world. First, I needed to let these folks know. On December 22, 2019, I came out to my new congregation. On that Sunday, I preached a shorter sermon than usual and Shelly joined me at the pulpit afterword. My daughters and son-in-law were present. I shared my truth. The love and acceptance from that awesome community were immediate and heartfelt and have never wavered.

That same afternoon, I posted the same message I shared in worship on Facebook to make it "Facebook official." Then, everyone would know, and I could be completely open about who I have always been. The support from my social media community was also amazing. Overwhelming actually. Many people shared touching loving comments of affirmation. I admit I still go back and read them sometimes. I didn't expect that everyone commenting would be supportive. I was ready to unfriend a few people that afternoon, but no need ever presented itself.

Coming out was the best and most difficult thing I have ever done. Admitting long buried and denied truth about who you are at your core is frightening. Not knowing how people who have been important in your life will react contributes to the delay of honesty. However, for me, honesty has been the great emancipator. During the first 55 years of my life, I had no idea how denying myself took a toll on my mental and physical health, my body, and my relationships. When I speak or write, "I am gay," it is so natural, and I feel so proud to stand in that truth.

I've thought about whether I wish I had been able to be honest earlier in my life. Growing up, I had no positive role model, image, example, or language around queerness. It was only a word that was used against me to humiliate me and remind me of my difference. I never thought about it being true back then. My church at the time and my family did not speak in anything but jokes, sneers, and condemnation about men like me. So, being gay didn't even enter my mind. I didn't even think about being gay as a possible explanation for my struggle. So, my answer is no, I don't wish things had been different. My journey is what it is. It is mine, and I am shaped by it. Due to the path my life took, I have a rich array of friendships and experiences. I would have missed out on this journey that has brought me some amazing and loving people, including my wife and daughters.

Twenty-Seven

FOUND & FREE

In 2019, I auditioned for and was accepted as the newest member of The Cincinnati Men's Chorus. It had been long enough following my voice therapy that I was ready to get back into singing in a choir. I missed it a great deal. There is nothing like the comradery and the connection made with people during rehearsals, along with the reliance on each other during a performance. I also believed this would be a good way to get to know other gay men and immerse myself in a part of the community.

That first rehearsal was overwhelming. The music was not easy, and there was a lot of it. I learned it had to be memorized, and there was choreography on top of trying to remember words and notes. Bruce, a fellow baritone was assigned as my chorus buddy to help me with questions and show me the ropes. Bruce checked in with me right away to see if I needed anything. He was funny and brought levity to the group of 80 men multiple times each Wednesday night.

Bruce told me after a couple of months that he had the task of introducing me to the whole group. I felt the familiar experience of my muscles tense. I began to feel some of the same sensations that had become part of me on a cellular level. The fear of being judged, which I always assumed would likely lead to rejection, was right there in that moment. The fear of being a disappointment. The good thing was that I didn't have to speak, just stand there while all of these men heard about me. That familiar feeling of holding my feelings in my body reminded me that I was not completely finished with this journey, and likely never will be. All I can hope for is to be better than I was, healthier than the day or year before, and continue to make progress. After all, I have lived this way for five decades. Not all of it will change quickly.

"So, are you partnered?" Bruce asked me while filing out his introduction questionnaire during a break at a rehearsal.

"Yes," I said, "for 36 years to my wife, Shelly."

"Oh, do tell," Bruce continued getting more serious. We were now attracting the attention of a few other guys sitting near. This chorus had historically been for gay men and it was an uncommon answer.

"I am living in a mixed orientation marriage. I came out about a year and a half ago, and we decided to stay together and make it work."

The response was always the same as it always was. "I've never heard of a mixed orientation marriage."

I usually respond with, "Look it up. It's a real thing."

Two weeks later, the rehearsal approached when Bruce was to introduce me. I was still nervous. The first hour and a half of rehearsal passed as usual, and it came time. One hundred and sixty eyes fixed on me standing in front of them as Bruce read through his information sheet.

He told them I was a pastor. That was another one that concerned me. I hadn't said that to many people there yet. The comments and jokes about religion in previous weeks reinforced my assumption that a pastor might not be all that welcomed. Bruce revealed my secret with a joke about the new church I started not being a cult. People laughed with us and not at me. That was one hurdle down.

Then he revealed the biggest news yet. I was married to a woman and making a mixed orientation marriage work while exploring what it meant to embrace being a gay man.

"I've learned something I didn't know tonight," the director said as Bruce and I took our seats.

Another question on Bruce's form was my favorite movie. When he asked me beforehand, I told him that I would have to get back to him. I love movies and see dozens each year. I was hard pressed to say what was my favorite. He asked me to consider a movie I return to and watch over and over. I told him earlier that evening my answer for that blank spot in his introduction.

"And Dale's favorite movie is 'The Devil Wears Prada'," Bruce stated. Heads nodded in affirmation.

That movie had come to mind when he first asked, but I found myself hesitating, "I can't say that movie. A guy wouldn't say that movie. I can't let them know that I watch that movie over and over."

But then it dawned on me. Yes, I can. I can say that. I can admit my favorite movie is about a woman who struggles to live up to the expectations of her boss, who is demanding and difficult, all of them working in the world of a women's fashion magazine. My favorite moment is when a coworker argues that Andrea doesn't really want the job since she just whines and complains about it rather than committing herself to what is required. I love that she does what's required, and she does it well. Through it all, Andrea discovers her true self and learns what is and is not important to her.

That night in choir rehearsal, I could stand in my truth in a group of men, no less, who totally got that answer, "The Devil Wears Prada." I came out of my hiding and told the truth, and it was great. And, no one laughed.

Before I sat down, I felt like I should clarify a few things. I stood back up and said to the group, "Bruce did a great job telling about me tonight. I just want to add, I was 55 when I finally was able to tell the truth to myself about who I am. When I told my wife, we decided we wanted to keep as much of our life as we could while making room for this reality. My wife loved me enough to give me permission to be myself."

They applauded.

Then and in the weeks to follow, men approached me to share their stories. One had cared for a terminally ill wife. "I didn't come out until she died." Another was a retired pastor finding strength and hope. "I deserve to be happy too, don't I?" I heard of children and grandchildren and marriages where divorce happened and the struggle to be authentic was met with pain.

I felt as if I had been given new life. I realized how important it was that I found my voice and could own it and appreciate it and use it.

I was included in a group of people who understood. I was part of a group who knew all about me, and they were accepting, even if they didn't understand how a gay man could continue a marriage to a woman after coming out.

I knew I would never be the same. It wasn't the only time I had felt that way during the course of my journey, and it will not be the last, I have realized I don't need to make others feel okay with who I am.

One of the first songs I rehearsed with the Men's Chorus was, "Make Them Hear You," from Ragtime. The words were striking to me, "Teach every child to raise his voice and then, my brothers, then will justice be demanded by ten million righteous men."

To all of those bullies who teased me as a kid, you were right. I am gay. I kind of wish I could have seen what you knew. It wouldn't have made anything easier. You taught me to have more compassion toward others than you showed me. I know the pain of being the object of jokes and what it feels like to think other people are laughing at you. I never want to do that to another human being.

The church I grew up in as a teen and young college student was full of people who gave me a foundation on which to build. I take issue with much of my experiences back then but not with the sincerity of those people, some of whom are still cherished people in my life to this day.

I left the United Methodist Church on June 30, 2019. After 30 years, I decided I wanted to be true to my belief that God's family was made up of every part of the human family. I wanted to live out my values of inclusion and felt that specific church wasn't going to allow that to happen any time soon. I also have come to realize that the system that governs the life of the people, especially pastors, in the United Methodist Church was based on shaming. I felt like someone in authority was always judging me or breathing down my neck, looking over my shoulder and second guessing my decisions. It was hard to live up to the pressure of increasing numbers of people and dollars. I wanted to be about much more than that and let numbers of people and dollars take care of themselves. I wanted to follow Jesus and lead people who wanted the same. I wanted to declare that I believed Jesus welcomed everyone to the widest grace and love imaginable. I wanted to shout how everyone should be celebrated for who they were created to be. I wanted to create a safe space for LGBTQ+ family members. So, I surrendered my ordination and set out on a new adventure.

The Open Table was born July 1, 2019, as a group of people started meeting together in parks and people's homes.

I was ordained by The Federation of Christian Ministries in October of 2019. The Federation of Christian Ministries was founded in 1968 by Roman Catholic priests. Their own history states the reason as: to give voice to priests looking for church reform, especially for optional celibacy. They have since been a haven for women priests in the Catholic tradition, LGBTQ+ clergy looking for places to be accepted, and many others.

During the retreat where I was ordained, I sat with people who were living out their faith in a variety of ways representing God's rainbow of promise to all humanity. There were pastors, chaplains, and musicians. There were men and women who had once belonged to a variety of faith traditions. There were gays and straight people, all sharing with each other, being honest, praying, eating and drinking at the communion table, proclaiming a new creation that reflects God in all her majesty. I was overwhelmed and moved to emotion during the retreat's closing worship.

We were asked to share our own ordination vows. Mine were:

God, who calls and equips me for this life,

I will trust you in all things knowing that you hold me in unimaginable love and grace.

I will be authentic and real.

I will be truthful to people, telling them that following Jesus is not about rules, theology, or an institution, but about relationships and putting flesh on the gospel.

I will not contribute to making more consumer Christians, but disciples who know Jesus.

I will be committed to the mission of God in the world and be open to my part in proclaiming the Kingdom's reality.

I will be agile in responding to your Spirit's movement and open to the possibilities you present.

***

For those who may wonder if the sexual abuse at the hands of the man and woman passing themselves off as my grandparents was a contributing factor to me being gay, I have had the same thought. The counseling for the abuse was prior to my coming out, so I was quite excited to grasp on to an explanation that would finally end my "struggle." I asked that question of my counselor. She said, your grandmother and grandfather both abused you, but you don't feel the same about a penis and a vagina. If that were true, you'd be attracted to them both. "Damn," I thought," She's right. I am gay. I have been for as long as I can recall."

Though much pain was caused by the people in my life as a child, I really do have some good memories as well. There were moments of laughter. Mamaw and Papaw were consistent, which wasn't something I had any other place in my life as a child. I have no memory that the abuse continued past the age of eight. For whatever reason it just seems to have stopped. Ramped up, however, was Mamaw's grip on my emotional soul.

My parents acted out of what they knew. I really don't blame them or hold any of my experiences over their heads. After their divorce and many years after the fact, I have been able to understand them and love them for what they are able to give. Each of us could expect no less or more from each other. That is especially true for my mom. I know she loves me. It is a love that she has learned how to express in some unhealthy ways from unhealthy people who smothered her childhood too. The same people who abused me are intricately linked to us both. So, we are alike in many ways, and that can and has caused conflict.

My dad is a man of strength and faithfulness. He is solid as a man who loves God. He can pray, let me tell you. When he says he prays for me, I actually know I am in good hands. He has made huge strides to show love to me and express that love. I cling to and cherish his progress in that regard. I could do no better than to imitate my dad.

Shelly has been at my side for decades and still stands right there. I could not have made this journey without her. There is no way I would be the authentic version of myself without her influence. We were brought together to help each other on this journey to be whole. We have not attained it completely but are way better than we were when we met at that Columbus Clippers game in 1983.

My sister has been a source of consistent and constant love. Our relationship has always been strong, and it continues to be.

My kids have been through so much with me (My youngest has come out as a transgender male since I began writing this book.). What turmoil I brought into our family at times as I attempted to push down and hold in all that was inside me. That's exhausting and impossible. A professor, David Seamands, in a seminary class for pastoral counseling said once, "If you keep pushing stuff to the basement of yourself, it will start to stink sooner or later." Beth and Kendel have loved me through it all. They have grown into awesome adults who still call their dad to talk.

Friends have been with me all along the way. Perplexed

at times, I'm sure, but still showing up and being present for me.

I love my family. I love the friends who have come through my life. I love my church community who takes risks with me and shows me love.

I didn't know the power of sharing my own story until I started to be honest. It's like that honesty allowed others to risk honesty themselves. I have heard so many painful stories and hope-filled dreams.

I had to do physical therapy recently for my back and shoulder. During those sessions I discovered, again, how tightly I have held my muscles and my entire body for so many years. That ever-present tension is now so much a part of me that I don't even recognize it until challenged to do so.

The physical therapist was holding my arm one appointment and said, "just relax your arm. Let me have it. Let it go limp."

I replied, "Oh, I can't do that. I have to think about that and intentionally let it happen."

It's the same old story, but now I can at least recognize it.

I have been awakened to myself. Truth is present in my consciousness. I have a voice that is uniquely mine. It is a voice that was dampened and silenced by a variety of circumstances with similar threads—abuse, manipulation, abandonment, mistrust. It took me decades to realize that, like each of us, I have a contribution to make to the world that no one else is able to make. My experiences, as do all of ours, shaped me and what I am able to produce.

That voice therapy session where I stood on a Good Friday afternoon, relaxing my throat muscles, allowing air to find its way out of my core, changed everything. I heard powerful deep sounds that filled the room. I have since carried them out into the world like opening a window to let out what can't be contained. Or, what just yearns to be free so it can spread everywhere the wind blows, or even just across the street.

I breathe in deeply, and I exhale.

Even though I will continue on this journey, I have already discovered so much more of my truth. In that discovery, I have embraced what I believe and who I am, not just what others have told me about myself and what is true. I now have the ability to stand in my wholeness.

Out of my deepest authentic me, I relax my throat muscles, open my mouth, clearing the way for my voice to come out, unforced, unencumbered, all on its own. That voice escapes my lips. This Easter, I stand to sing with fullness and depth, "Love's redeeming work is done. Alleluia! Fought the fight the battle won. Alleluia!"

About the Author

After serving more than 30 years as a United Methodist pastor, Dale Lykins realized the institutional church he had given so much to was not aligned with his values.

In 2019, Dale began a new chapter. He helped establish an inclusive and affirming church, The Open Table, where people are accepted no matter who they are or where they are on their life journey. Dale also came out as gay during this time, which solidified his commitment to building a church community that accepts all people.

Dale also pursues his mission of connecting and helping others live authentic, honest lives through speaking engagements, one-on-one coaching, and writing. While his faith is part of his own story, he welcomes and celebrates differences of backgrounds and faiths.

Dale is a native Ohioan and a graduate of The Ohio State University and Asbury Theological Seminary. He and his wife, Shelly, are in a mixed-orientation marriage. They live in the Cincinnati, Ohio, area and have a daughter, a son, and two grandsons. Dale is ordained with the Federation of Christian Ministries.

To connect with Dale Lykins

- View pictures and updates from the story found in Hush, Child
- Subscribe to The Unlearning Blog
- Book Dale for a speaking engagement
- Sign-up for coaching with Dale

Go to **www.DaleLykins.com**